Texas

•San Antonio

•Refugio

• Corpus Christi

• Sarita

• Laguna Madre

City•

edo•

McAllen•

◉ Brownsville

Gu
of
Mex

Hidalgo•
nterrey•

• Tampico

an Miguel
elia

• Mexico City

• Veracruz

• Puebla

The ENCHILADA QUEEN COOKBOOK

SYLVIA CASARES

with Dotty Griffith

The ENCHILADA QUEEN COOKBOOK

Enchiladas, Fajitas, Tamales, and More Classic Recipes from Texas-Mexico Border Kitchens

ST. MARTIN'S GRIFFIN ❧ NEW YORK

www.stmartins.com

Designed by Ralph Fowler / rlfdesign

Photographs by Rick Turner, Alex Martinez, Nancy Aidée González, and Gina Pizzini

The Library of Congress Cataloging-in-Publication Data is available upon request.

ISBN 978-1-250-08291-6 (hardcover)
ISBN 978-1-250-08292-3 (e-book)

Our books may be purchased in bulk for promotional, educational, or business use. Please contact your local bookseller or the Macmillan Corporate and Premium Sales Department at 1-800-221-7945, extension 5442, or by e-mail at MacmillanSpecialMarkets@macmillan.com.

First Edition: November 2016

10 9 8 7 6 5 4 3 2 1

This book is dedicated to my parents and brothers, my dear
children, my close friends, and the many loyal and very
supportive customers who have cheered me on year after
year and have embraced my restaurants from the very start.

A special thank-you to my parents, Severita and
Everardo Casares, most loving parents who gave me the
foundation to do all I have done in my life. And, to my
very dearest companion and my strongest resource, my
faith in God, which gives me wisdom, encouragement,
and protection to achieve this lifetime goal.

CONTENTS

CHAPTER 4

Enchilada Queen Wisdom 42

or Why Sylvia Is "the Queen"

CHAPTER 5

Salsas, Appetizers, and Snacks 83

CHAPTER 10

Enchilada Queen Sweet Endings   180

CHAPTER 11

Sipping with the Enchilada Queen   198

FOREWORD

She wasn't always the Enchilada Queen. Before she appeared on the Food Channel, and graced the cover of the *Houston Chronicle*'s Dining Guide every other week, and made *Texas Monthly*'s list of top Mexican restaurants in Houston, and *USA Today* ranked Sylvia's as one of "Ten Great Mexican Restaurants in the US," she was just my older sister. Everyone has to start somewhere.

Sylvia Maria Casares entered the world as the third child of Everardo and Severa Casares, neither of whom descended from royal lineage but did what they could to provide us with a stable and loving home. We lived on the east side of Brownsville, Texas, in a small three-bedroom clapboard house with light-blue trim and a carport that leaned to the right. An enormous grapefruit tree reigned in the backyard and held its ground when Hurricane Beulah whipped through in 1968. Back then, Brownsville was a town of about fifty thousand people, with only one high school, a junior college, a small airport (which is still a small airport today), and two bridges that connected us to Matamoros, where we would go sometimes for groceries or a haircut or something more involved like a tailored suit or a wedding gown. Our mother worked in Brownsville as a clerk at HEB,

and later at another grocery store called El Centro. Our father worked as a tick inspector for the USDA, a job that also required that he patrol the Rio Grande on horseback, watching

Sylvia with her brothers, 1966

for stray livestock. When he came home for dinner there was the *arroz con pollo*, there were the *calabacitas*, there were the *taquitos*, there were the fresh-made flour tortillas. And there was Sylvia watching our mother prepare these meals, as my sister had also once upon a time watched our grandmother, Mamá Grande, do.

Later, when Sylvia moved away to attend the University of Texas at Austin and earn a degree in home economics, with the intent of teaching high school, on the weekends she would take the long six-hour drive back home to Brownsville and, again, watch my mother cook. After graduating, instead of teaching she took a job in the test kitchen at Uncle Ben's Rice in Houston, where she watched and learned to cook meticulously, with an emphasis on taste. Still later, when she went into food sales for companies like Heinz and Sara Lee and Kraft, she watched how restaurant kitchens worked from the inside out, where they splurged and where they cut corners and how this affected the final taste of the food. It was this collection of ingredients— the down-home cooking of our mother and grandmother, the analytics of the corporate test kitchen, and the understanding of how a successful restaurant operated, starting with the mom-and-pop outfits all the way to the chains—that led Sylvia to take several leaps of faith, from watching to doing, from learning to experimenting, from cooking to serving.

It's easy to look at her success now and think it was simple enough. But she's had her ups and downs like every other businessperson. And she's had her setbacks, some of which she will talk about in more detail. Today, her customers know her as the Enchilada Queen, but very few of these people were actually around back in 1995, when she started her first restaurant along Highway 90 in Rosenberg, in a tiny place that the previous owners had painted a certain shade of pink that made it look less like a Mexican restaurant and more like an outlet store for Mary Kay. And later, after she had some success and moved the business to the big city, there were still several years when she struggled to get noticed while she was located in a lonely shopping strip, tucked in between a nameless donut shop and a place called Puppy World.

Now here she is almost twenty years later, the Enchilada Queen. And here you are, holding the book that contains many of the recipes that got her here. But will this make you the Enchilada Queen? Well, there's already one of those in Texas and I don't think she's stepping down anytime soon. On the other hand, with some careful reading and a little prep time there's no reason you can't be your own family's Enchilada Queen. Or King.

—Oscar Casares,
January 2016

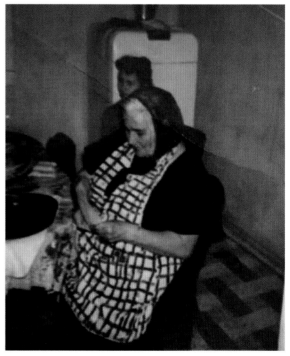

Above: My maternal grandmother, Manuela, with her mother and father, Inez and Julian, and her sister, Juliana, in 1901.

Above right: My parents, Everardo and Severa Casares, on their wedding day, March 22, 1939, in Donna, Texas. My mother was sixteen and my father was twenty-five.

Right: Grandmother Sarita making tamales on Christmas Eve in 1960.

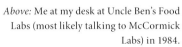

Above: Me at my desk at Uncle Ben's Food Labs (most likely talking to McCormick Labs) in 1984.

Above right: My First Communion.

Right: My mother and me, aged three, at Easter in 1956 in Donna, Texas.

HOW I BECAME THE ENCHILADA QUEEN

I didn't start out to be the Enchilada Queen. It just happened: a spontaneous coronation that took me by surprise.

When I was first called the Enchilada Queen, I thought it made me sound like I was getting "too big for my britches." Then I realized that the title given to me by local food media meant that Sylvia's Enchilada Kitchen was what I always wanted it to be: the Best. *H Texas Magazine* dubbed me the Enchilada Queen in 2006. I've been proud to wear the crown ever since.

That was the culmination of the culinary journey I've been on since I was ten. That's how old I was when I started learning to cook by watching my grandmother and my mother. I've always been a high-energy person who wanted to help, especially my parents. My mother worked, and I liked to surprise her with dinner ready for the family when she came home. I imitated my grandmother and mother to learn how to cook. Many of the homestyle recipes in chapter 7 I learned from her. They are recipes that my three brothers and I grew up on in South Texas and that my children loved when they ate at home instead of the restaurant.

I was a "helper" kid and sort of hyperactive. Even though I saw cooking as a favor to the family, my mother worried when I wanted to do it alone. She was afraid I'd burn myself. But I kept cooking and the family kept eating. And I didn't burn myself . . . too badly.

As a student, I wasn't terribly academic, but I got As and Bs. And I loved to sew. That put me on the path to studying home economics at the big state university in Austin. The University of Texas was such a faraway place for me as a kid who grew up along the Texas-Mexico border in Brownsville. Three hundred miles is a long way no matter how you measure it, but in my world at the time, Austin and The University felt like a different planet.

Still, I did just fine and was ready to graduate with a home economics degree. Now it was time to get a job as a teacher. After all, that was a career open to women. As a wife and mother of a three-year-old, teaching seemed like my best pathway, but while doing my student teaching, I got a call from a friend about a job opening at Uncle Ben's Rice in Houston. That phone call changed my life.

I followed up on the tip and found out how much better I'd be paid at Uncle Ben's than as a teacher. I went after that job and got a phone interview. Next thing, I was working in the research lab at one of the state's largest food companies in Texas' largest city. The reason I got hired at Uncle Ben's was because I had a bachelor's of science degree from the University of Texas that included chemistry and microbiology.

With that background in science, I went to work in the research lab and then the test kitchens and then the product development lab. That's how I learned to develop recipes with precision. I'm big on measuring. From my college and work experience, I know how important it is to get the right chemistry for optimum flavor and consistency. I train my staff to measure everything right down to the salt. We don't just do recipes "to taste." Of course, we taste and adjust, but everything is measured. That has built the Sylvia's Enchilada Kitchen reputation for high quality and consistency, and it's why the recipes in this book really work.

After three years in the test kitchens and seven years in the lab at Uncle Ben's, I was ready for something else. I took a University of Houston class on changing careers. That helped me decide I would leave at the end of 1986. I changed gears completely and left a secure, well-paying job for something that would take me toward the career I was meant for but didn't yet know. Walking away from the golden handcuffs that my job represented was one of the scariest days of my life. Sobbing and fearful as I left for the last time, I was determined to do something more with my life than work in a test lab.

I went to work—on commission—for Kraft selling their products to restaurants and food service outlets. That's where I first started learning about how restaurants operate. Not surprisingly here in the Houston area, many of my customers were Mexican restaurants. That's when I began to realize that the cuisine I'd grown up on wasn't something everybody knew. Others might find it exotic, new, interesting, and delicious. The seed had been planted for me to one day open my own restaurant.

The first few months in the new job were awful. There were days I didn't sell one case of anything. But I kept at it and did well enough that eighteen months later, I landed a more promising job selling for a gourmet frozen soup company. I worked hard, moving up through the ranks and getting better jobs along the way. By the time I was in my early forties, I held a high-paying position with a high-profile national food company that required a lot of travel.

Again I determined it was time for a change. I was set to have dinner with four male colleagues after a food show in San Antonio. I arrived ten minutes late and found them sitting at a table for four. They barely looked up from their conversation and cocktails, and told me to pull up a chair at the corner. That's when I knew I was fed up with the travel and what was, at the time, a very male-oriented industry. Even though I was successful, I still had trouble—literally—getting a seat at the table.

That was about the time when my husband mentioned a restaurant for sale in the small town of Rosenberg just outside Houston. I'd begun to think about owning a restaurant when I first left Uncle Ben's and got familiar with the business. The time seemed right, so we jumped at the opportunity. Most of my friends couldn't believe I was leaving a good job as regional sales manager to take over a "little bitty Mexican restaurant."

In 1995 we cashed in part of my 401K and bet most of our life savings on my dream and that "little bitty Mexican restaurant." That's how my restaurant career began. I guess a part of me has always been a daredevil. After a few months becoming familiar with customers and employees, I determined what I could do to rebuild and improve the menu. One dish at a time, I analyzed each recipe, improved the techniques, insisted on the freshest ingredients, and reformulated the food and the kitchen procedure. My mantra became, "No shortcuts when it comes to flavor." I can be such a perfectionist that I spent ten months improving the recipe for just one of my enchilada dishes.

With lots of regular customers, word of mouth spread and the business grew and grew. That's when I knew I could make it in the big city if I could figure out a way to set my restaurant apart from Houston's other eleven thousand eateries.

Most Tex-Mex restaurants serve enchiladas, but few make them a signature. As always,

I went all in. Naming my restaurant Sylvia's Enchilada Kitchen highlighted my best dishes but added pressure to maintain a high level of quality.

I debuted my first Houston location in 1998. I'd recently divorced, and the Rosenberg location split up along with the marriage. Today, I have three Sylvia's Enchilada Kitchen locations in H-town, as it is known locally.

My first year in the big city was tough. I'd opened in a location that wasn't very visible. After a year of barely breaking even, I thought about selling out. But I've never quit at anything. Instead I circled the wagons and fought to build my business. I leased a nearby billboard to tell the 100,000 drivers that daily passed my way—but didn't know I was there—about Sylvia's Enchilada Kitchen. My brother, Oscar, a former advertising exec turned professor and novelist, wrote the copy: "The Best Enchiladas in Houston Are Also the Hardest to Find." Below those words a

big arrow pointed toward the restaurant. Six months later, my restaurant was exploding with customers.

Since then, I have opened two more locations and teach cooking classes at my flagship restaurant. Teaching cooking classes has taught me a lot about what my customers want and like. Three kinds of guests frequent my restaurants:

1. Those who love great food. They read, study, keep up on culinary trends. They insist on authentic, quality dishes. They have excellent palates. My customers memorize the flavors of my food on their tongues. Bottom line is that foodies love my food.

2. People with roots in South Texas. They recognize and love the authentic regional flavors that are so hard to find anywhere but along the Rio Grande border. About 50 percent of my customers come in craving something, and that's what they order.

3. *Amigos* of Mexican descent. They are folks who have eaten this kind of food, especially as children. When you've eaten a food over a lifetime, you recognize it immediately. One taste and you know when it is right or wrong. Many who attend my classes are sisters coming together because their mothers and grandmothers didn't write down the recipes.

The success of my restaurants, catering business, and cooking classes, plus constant requests from customers, cooking students, and food media convinced me I should write a cookbook. It took a life-altering experience to convince me to take the time to write it.

In March 2012, I had a near-death experience that made me realize life is fragile and there were numerous things I wanted to do but had not been able to get to. I realized that I was way out of balance in my work life and that the cookbook I'd always wanted to write needed to get written and published. During my time of recovery and reflection, I documented my new goals. Then I got really busy upon my return to work, and here I am today.

Love made me write this book. I'm talking about the love that goes into cooking the timeless recipes of my heritage. These are the treasured and delicious dishes that came from my grandmother's kitchen and my mother's, and, now, from my kitchen to yours.

It was a passion of mine to write this cookbook because I have a conviction that these are "true recipes" that must be preserved. I was concerned that many of the flavors and techniques of the Texas-Mexico border kitchens could be forgotten to modernity and busy lives. I didn't want these recipes to be lost to my children and their children. These recipes have the power to bridge generations. They connect my parents to the generations before them and to my children and theirs.

What was sparked by a concern has become a work of love and pride in the preservation of 125 authentic recipes that create flavor markers for the delicious traditions I took for granted as a child, which now I am dedicated to keeping alive forever. The authentic character of the recipes in this book has been safeguarded, and the traditional techniques have been adapted to modern equipment and time constraints. Enchilada Queen recipes are "real," made accessible and practical for today's cooks. When you prepare them for your family and friends, you'll see what I mean about the generations of love passed down in these recipes.

CHAPTER 1

BORDER CUISINE

Eating Along the Rio Grande

When it comes to food, there are no boundaries. Especially with Tex-Mex, America's first fusion cuisine. What is Tex-Mex? It is a blending of Mexican ingredients, traditions, and flavors with the ingredients, traditions, and flavors American settlers brought as they moved into the area that would eventually come to be known as Texas. In the early 1800s, most of that territory was claimed by Mexico. Definitely more Mex than Tex at the time.

There's a long history and tradition of blurred cultural and culinary lines between Texas and Mexico. Sometimes that means there are different names for the same thing. Texans think of the river along the border as the Rio Grande, while Mexicans call the same flowing water Rio Bravo. On the other hand, a word may have different connotations, depending on where it is spoken. Both Mexicans and Texans speak and eat enchiladas. Yet the basic dish called enchiladas has different fillings and sauces depending on where they're made. In Mexico, enchiladas are more likely to be filled with chicken, white cheese, or pork. In Texas, beef or yellow cheese are the favored fillings. Also in Mexico,

tortillas are traditionally made with ground dried corn. When European settlers arrived, they adapted the Mexican tortilla technique to use white flour. Is the chicken or beef enchilada, the flour or the corn tortilla, more Tex-Mex or more Mex-Tex? They all are. That's the beauty of this blended cuisine.

I point this out to show that the only hard line between Texas and Mexico is the manmade boundary drawn on maps. And even that has changed over the years. At one time, the Nueces River, about a hundred miles inside what is now Texas, was *la frontera*. It wasn't until 1848, after the Mexican-American War, that the Rio Grande (aka *Rio Bravo del Norte*) was established as the border.

That's the backstory on *mi tierra* (my land) and the biculinary, bicultural world I know. I grew up in Brownsville, the very southern tip of Texas. On the other side of the river lies Matamoros, Mexico. I have family ancestry on both sides. During my childhood and until the horrors of 9/11 made border security a national imperative, people routinely traveled back and forth without passports. No different than travel between Brownsville and another Texas city,

McAllen, only not as far. So did residents of Laredo and Nuevo Laredo, El Paso and Juarez, and other cross-border sibling cities. Each pair is separated by a river, but joined by bridges, tradition, business, geography, climate, language, family, and friendship. The culinary traditions blend and meld as smoothly as *chile con queso*, the staple cheese dip of Tex-Mex. Yet there are subtle differences. Made in Mexico, what we call *queso* for short uses white cheese. On the Texas side, yellow cheese dominates.

I think of the cuisine on both sides of the river as "border cuisine," a reflection of the land and people who populate both sides of a major river that happens to be an international border. They share the same climate, land, plants, and animals. At the same time, there are differences. Some are ethnic, some are national, some are tradition-based or influenced by historic events. The common thread, however, is a hard-scrabble, close-to-the-earth way of cooking and eating that uses what's available to the best advantage. There have, of course, been other factors.

On the Mexico side, French and Spanish colonial influences greatly inspired many culinary practices, such as flour tortillas, *tortas* (French baguette or Spanish *bolillo* sandwiches) and flan; *crème brûlée* in France, *crema Catalan* in Spain.

On the Texas side, settlers with German,

Section of Rio Grande, close to the Gulf of Mexico.

English, and Irish heritages, as well as southern tastes, melded their traditions with the food as well. Fondness for flour tortillas is a key example. But so is the emphasis on beef, as many of the American settlers came to build a life as cattle ranchers.

Tex-Mex is a beautiful blend of cuisines and cultures. Sometimes people tell me they love my food because it isn't Tex-Mex. They're mistaken, because what I cook *is* Tex-Mex, made the way people make it all along both sides of the border. Some of my dishes may be more Mexican, others more Texan, but they are almost always Tex-Mex, at least as I know it. Sadly, what is often called Tex-Mex is mass-produced, commercial food; heavy,

even greasy, and varying shades of brown layered with too much bright yellow cheese. If that's all you know of Tex-Mex, no wonder you dismiss Tex-Mex and "the enchilada plate" as a gooey brown blob.

That's not what the way I cook. Whether in my restaurant or in my home, I use only the freshest and highest quality ingredients to make dishes from scratch the traditional way, with a few, well-considered exceptions. At my students' request, I've finally given in to using convenient canned pinto beans in the recipe for refried beans that I teach in my cooking classes. (At the restaurant, though, we still start with dried pinto beans.) I don't believe canned beans sacrifice too much flavor

for the amount of convenience gained for my students. That's a good trade.

In my restaurants, I've used enchiladas to explore the sauces and ingredients that reflect Hispanic cooking traditions on both sides of the Texas-Mexico border. I grew up eating honest homegrown cuisine influenced by centuries of tradition. That's what I know and love. In this cookbook, I go beyond enchiladas. I share my recipes and techniques for Tex-Mex and Mexican classics, including nachos and *flautas*; tacos and fajitas; tamales as well as South Texas–style mesquite-grilled beef, chicken, fish, quail, and *cabrito* (baby goat). Recipes include many of my signature restaurant sides including the Mexican classic, *rajas poblanos con crema* (creamed poblano chiles) and basic Rio Grande–style refried beans. Of course, there's a recipe for my customers' favorite dessert, chocolate *tres leches* (three milks) cake.

These recipes are written with the same attention to detail and precision learned in commercial test kitchens and that I have trained my staff to use in my restaurants. They have been adapted to home kitchen amounts, techniques, modern ingredients, and equipment. That's why my classes are so popular and successful. I've translated restaurant recipes into recipes for cooks at home. I don't horde professional secrets. What you get with this cookbook are fail-safe recipes that reflect the flavors, ingredients, and dishes that have been prepared and eaten on both sides of the Rio Grande, or *Rio Bravo*, for hundreds of years. Many are just as you would get in my restaurants. Some are recipes that I reserve for home and family. All are authentic and easy to replicate.

I want this book to grow respect for and appreciation of the oldest regional cooking style in the United States, Tex-Mex, America's first fusion cuisine. I draw on recipes from both sides of the river since Mexico is anything but foreign to those who live just north of the border. Likewise Texas is not unknown to those who live to the south. There's a long history of interplay. Nothing symbolizes *mi tierra* better than the cuisine.

My brother, Oscar, calls me a purist. That's his kind way of saying I'm old-fashioned. And I'm proud of it. Whether you call this cuisine Tex-Mex, Mex-Tex, Border, or Mexican, it's a reflection of a way of life in which culinary traditions are blind to everything but flavor.

One of the best ways to express this is with a map, a mural in my restaurants. This reflects the geographic range and some of the regional inspirations for my cuisine and the recipes in this book. The core of my cuisine is a set of fourteen sauces that I have developed over the years. Made daily in each restaurant, these sauces represent the cooking traditions along the Texas-Mexico border as well as in other parts of Texas and Mexico.

Some dishes, like the Sarita enchilada (*calabacita*—squash—enchiladas with *queso* and cream sauce), are named after small Texas towns. So is the Refugio plate (cheese enchiladas with chili gravy), and Crystal City (spinach enchiladas reflecting the town's reputation as a major south Texas vegetable growing area). The El Paso entrée features stacked, not rolled, enchiladas for which the far West Texas town and New Mexico are known. Dishes named for locales in Mexico include Mexico City–style chicken enchiladas, *mole* from Puebla, and Gulf Coast port Tampico shrimp enchiladas.

CHAPTER 2

THE FOUNDATION

Tortillas, Basics, Flavor Tricks

The building blocks of Rio Grande cuisine are tortillas and key spices, including the Tex-Mex Holy Trinity, a seasoning paste of cumin, black pepper, and fresh garlic. I'll introduce you to them by sharing my philosophy about recipe development. It is both a science and an art.

Almost every recipe in this book has a story about when I first experienced it, what inspired it, how I developed it. Since many of my recipes are actually classics for which a standard exists, I often experience some anxiety when developing a recipe, knowing that there will be customers and foodies whose expert palates will know if my recipe is "real" and whether the dishes are exceptionally flavored and expertly prepared.

Since my goal is always to earn a perfect grade of "10," I take a very pragmatic approach when developing a recipe. I put on my lab coat, pull out my note pad, and go to work!

One example of my process was the challenge of creating my formula for marinating beef fajitas. During the early years of my first restaurant, my focus and passion were dedicated to the enchilada side of my menu. It is a natural human tendency to gravitate toward things that come easily or naturally. Sauces and gravies are my favorites for sure.

So when it came to fajitas I needed to do some research. I had no idea where to begin, so I started by studying every recipe I could find to start to understand what other cooks were doing to flavor and tenderize beef for fajitas. I tested these recipes and found the results unacceptable. I found that all too often the beef flavor of fajitas was lost to the flavor of the marinades and the strips of skirt steak weren't tenderized enough. Though I'd never eaten much beef, especially steaks, my goal was for my fajitas to be tender and taste like a great steak.

It took two years, off and on, to reach my lofty goal with beef fajitas. What really spurred me on was one day a very loyal customer, who is also a big foodie, very kindly pulled me aside and brought to my attention that my enchiladas were a "10" but my fajitas were noticeably lower on the food rating scale. It was no surprise, but, nevertheless, a bit embarrassing to be reminded that my fajitas were an afterthought—second in priority to my enchiladas.

That reenergized me to finish my quest for a great fajita marinade. Eventually I achieved my goal after months of trial and error and dozens of "taste panels" with my staff. I have learned through all these years that setting a goal, then applying patience and perseverance to the development process, will birth a winning recipe.

Be assured that the basic recipes in this chapter, and throughout the book, have undergone the same rigorous development process.

Equipment

Throughout this book, recipes have lists of special equipment needed to complete the recipes. This is a list of the tools mentioned throughout the book; specialized equipment (like the *comal, molcajete,* tamale steamer, and tortilla warmer) can be ordered at mexgrocer .com if you're unable to find the items in a store near you.

Of particular importance are tools for blending dried chiles, spices, and cooked vegetables to make smooth sauces. Traditionally, a stone *molcajete* and pestle was the way to get this done. Today, a blender, food processor, mini-chopper, and spice grinder achieve the result quicker and with considerably less effort.

- Blender
- Board for pastry and chopping
- Charcoal or gas grill
- Cocktail shaker
- *Comal* or griddle
- Electric mixer
- Food handlers' gloves for working with fresh and dried chiles

- Food processor
- Heatproof gloves to handle hot food while grilling
- Immersion blender
- Large saucepans, Dutch ovens, stockpots, skillets
- Long tongs for grilling
- Mallet or small hammer
- *Molcajete* or mortar and pestle
- Mini-chopper
- Spice or coffee grinder
- Tamale steamer
- Tortilla warmer

Ingredients

Many of the foods used over and over in this book are indigenous to Mexico and the Southwest. Many are widely available. Put them on your weekly shopping list if you're cooking and eating the Rio Grande way. See Resource List (page 213) and information boxes throughout the book for additional information about where to get ingredients and how to prep them.

- Avocados, Mexican preferred, if in season
- Chiles, dried: arbol, guajillo, pasilla, pequin
- Chiles, fresh: jalapeño, poblano, serrano
- Chocolate
- Cinnamon, Mexican preferred for some dishes
- Cumin seeds
- Corn, fresh and frozen
- *Crema*

- Epazote, fresh or dried
- *María galletas* (tea biscuits or cookies)
- *Masa harina* (instant corn flour)
- Mexican oregano, dried
- *Nopales* (chopped cactus pads)
- *Piloncillo* (Mexican cone sugar)
- Tomatillos
- Vanilla: pure extract, not imitation, authentic Mexican vanilla preferred

Enchilada Queen Tortilla Bootcamp

Whether corn or flour, tortillas are icons of border dishes and mealtimes. No Rio Grande meal, from breakfast through dinner, is complete without some kind of tortilla or variation thereon.

Rio Grande cuisine has for centuries relied on the corn tortilla. As a bread. As a wrapper. As a nutrition booster. Corn tortillas, when eaten with beans, add up to a complete protein and increase the absorbability of important minerals like iron. Pre-Columbian cultures were into corn tortillas hundreds, possibly thousands, of years before Europeans arrived with wheat flour. Eventually tortillas were adapted to use wheat flour as well.

In Tortilla Bootcamp, we start with basic corn tortillas and work our way through to flour tortillas.

Before plastic wrap and tortilla presses, making corn tortillas was a strictly by-hand endeavor. Today, making fresh corn tortillas is tricky even using a tortilla press but still much easier. Imagine the skill and time it took to produce dozens of corn tortillas, shaping them by hand, for big families or work crews and ranch hands.

To make corn tortillas, buy a good-quality tortilla press. It should be heavy metal, not plastic. You'll need to cut pieces of plastic wrap slightly larger than the surface of the tortilla press. This keeps the dough from sticking to the press.

Freshly pressed tortillas are very fragile and should be cooked immediately after shaping. Once cooked, they hold well in a tortilla warmer or towel-lined bowl or basket while you shape and cook your way through the dough.

Tortillas cook best on well-seasoned cast-iron griddles called *comals* that have been used and loved by several generations. But all of us have to start somewhere. If you buy—instead of inheriting—a *comal*, make sure it is cast iron or heavy steel. And season it well before using.

The temperature of the *comal* or griddle is critical for proper cooking. The temperature

How to season a new cast-iron *comal*

Scrub a new *comal* or cast-iron skillet and dry completely. Generously rub vegetable oil into the surface and place in a cold oven. Bring the oven temperature to 350°F. Turn off the heat and allow the *comal* to cool completely in the oven. Repeat oiling and baking three times before using.

of the surface should be about 400°F so the tortilla is marked with light brown spots after about 15 seconds.

If the grill is not hot enough, the tortillas will take longer to cook, and will harden or dry out before the light brown spots appear. If the temperature is too hot, the outside of the tortilla will burn while the interior remains doughy.

Use handmade fresh corn tortillas for tacos or as bread at the table. Delicious as they are, handmade corn tortillas are too thick for successful enchiladas. Rely on top-quality, fresh factory-made corn tortillas to make good enchiladas.

My corn tortillas require three ingredients: *masa harina* (instant corn flour); a little wheat flour; and salt moistened with water to form *masa*, dough. I add a bit of flour because the gluten helps the tortillas hold together. If you want to go gluten free, just omit the flour. Once the dough is the right consistency, form small balls of *masa* to press between the plates of a tortilla press lined with plastic wrap to prevent sticking. Flat discs of *masa* are "baked" on a hot flat griddle known as a *comal*. Just-cooked corn tortillas hold well in a tortilla warmer.

The stuff of which tortillas are made

I make corn tortillas with *masa harina* (instant corn flour). Before fresh corn becomes corn flour it undergoes a process called nixtamalization. Whole kernels are soaked and cooked in an alkaline solution, usually limewater, to produce nixtamal. Whole-kernel nixtamal is also known as *posole* or hominy. Ground fresh nixtamal becomes dough for tortillas, though it is seldom used in this form because it "sours" quickly. Dried and ground nixtamal is *masa harina* (instant corn flour), easily stored in bags, to which water is added to make tortilla dough.

The alkaline soaking process and the resulting chemical change make the difference between dried corn ground into meal—that is, cornmeal—and *masa harina*. Cornmeal without an additional ingredient such as flour will not form dough. *Masa harina*, when mixed with water, forms a pliable dough.

Handmade Corn Tortillas

Making corn tortillas requires practice and a heavy-duty tortilla press. Inexpensive models, some made of plastic, won't do the trick. It takes a fair amount of pressure to get thin tortillas, and flimsy presses break easily and often. If you're going to make corn tortillas, invest in a good-quality cast-iron press.

Makes 16 (6-inch) tortillas

Special Equipment

- Heavy cast-iron tortilla press
- Heavy cast-iron *comal* or griddle
- Tortilla warmer

2 cups *masa harina* (instant corn flour; Maseca brand preferred; see below)

3 tablespoons all-purpose flour (optional)

¼ teaspoon salt

In a medium bowl, combine the *masa*, flour (if using), and salt. Using your hands or a wooden spoon, mix well to blend.

Add 1½ cups water and mix until all the ingredients are well blended.

Knead for about 30 seconds, until the dough forms a firm but very pliable ball.

If the dough is too dry, add 2 to 3 tablespoons additional water.

Divide the dough into 16 golf ball–size rounds. Place in a large, clean bowl and cover with a damp towel or plastic wrap.

Preheat a *comal* or griddle over medium-high heat. The *comal* is ready when water sprinkled on the hot surface "dances." The temperature should be around 400°F.

Before cooking the tortillas, use a balled-up paper towel to apply a light coat of vegetable oil to the surface of the preheated *comal*.

(continued)

About *masa harina*

Maseca brand is the main label for *masa harina*, instant corn flour. Maseca so dominates the market that many people use the brand name in a generic way, just as some people say "Coke" when they mean any carbonated cola beverage.

Handmade Corn Tortillas *(continued)*

Using a tortilla press, place one piece of plastic wrap on the bottom plate. Place a dough ball in the center and press down with your hand to flatten to about 2 inches in diameter.

Center a second piece of plastic over the flattened dough and press down with the top side of the press. Press until the tortilla is about 6 inches in diameter.

Lift the tortilla off the press and carefully peel the plastic off one side. Turn the tortilla into your other hand. Peel off the second piece of plastic. Flip the tortilla onto the hot *comal.* (Veteran tortilla makers flip tortillas with their fingers. This requires a great deal of experience and desensitized fingertips. Not recommended that you try this at home!)

Cook the tortilla for about 15 seconds; then flip it over using a spatula. (This step is very important to set the dough.)

After flipping, cook the tortilla for about 1 minute, then flip again. Cook for another 1 minute. Place the cooked tortilla in a tortilla warmer or a bowl covered with a towel.

Repeat the process, oiling the *comal* as needed, until all the tortillas are pressed and cooked.

Handmade Flour Tortillas

Fresh, handmade flour tortillas are one of the great examples of cross-cultural culinary pollination. Somewhere between a crêpe and a pancake though shaped with dough instead of poured batter, the flour tortilla is a wonder of migration and adaptation.

The absolute best flour tortillas are made with lard—*manteca*—and Pioneer White Wings flour from an old San Antonio company, just like my mother and grandmother made them in South Texas. Since lard fell out of favor because of health concerns, I have always made flour tortillas at home and the restaurants with a high-quality vegetable shortening. Although lard has made a comeback in terms of its nutritional reputation at the expense of hydrogenated vegetable products like shortening, many customers, especially those who are vegetarian, prefer tortillas without lard so I continue to make them that way. If you get good enough at making flour tortillas, try them with lard.

Flour tortilla dough can be held at room temperature for 4 to 6 hours, as long as it's tightly covered so it doesn't dry out. For best results, do not refrigerate the dough, as the overall quality of the tortilla will diminish.

For "make-ahead tortillas," lightly cook each one and place on a cool surface. Place the tortillas in a plastic bag with a zipper, refrigerate for up to 2 weeks, and use as you go. Since the tortillas are

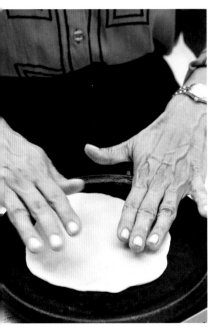

1. To make a flour tortilla, place the flattened tortilla on the hot comal. 2. Turn the tortilla when bubbles appear.
3. Press it onto the comal and cook for 2 minutes longer.

Handmade Flour Tortillas *(continued)*

only lightly cooked, you will need to fire up your *comal* or griddle to finish cooking. Place them on the hot surface until they are warm and puff slightly. These tortillas will be as tender and delicious as freshly cooked as long as they are stored in the sealed bag and aren't allowed to dry out.

Please, do not ruin your precious handmade flour tortillas by reheating in a microwave. The result is a rubbery texture. You'll be sorry you went to the trouble to make them if you zap to reheat.

Makes 12 (6-inch) tortillas

Special Equipment

- Heavy cast-iron *comal* or griddle
- Pastry or cutting board
- Rolling pin
- Tortilla warmer

2¼ cups all-purpose flour

1 teaspoon salt

4 teaspoons baking powder

½ cup vegetable shortening (Crisco preferred) or lard

¾ cup very warm (105 to 115°F) whole milk

Vegetable oil for cooking

In a medium bowl, combine 2 cups of the flour, the salt, and baking powder. Using a pastry cutter, blend in the shortening. Continue to blend in the fat until the mixture resembles coarse cornmeal.

Add the very warm milk to the flour mixture. Using your hands or a wooden spoon, gently blend to make a soft dough, kneading a few times. The dough should not be sticky. If it is, add a little flour. If the dough is a little stiff, add more milk, 1 tablespoon at a time. Do not overwork the dough.

When the dough is the right consistency, cover with plastic wrap and set aside for at least 1 hour and up to 6 hours.

Shape the dough into twelve rounds about the size of golf balls. Cover with towels until ready to roll out tortillas.

Preheat a *comal* or griddle over medium-high heat. The griddle is ready when water sprinkled on the hot surface "dances." The temperature should be around 400°F.

Sprinkle the remaining ¼ cup flour on a pastry or cutting board. Roll each ball in the flour to cover entirely.

Using a rolling pin, roll each piece of dough into a round ⅛ inch thick and 6 inches in diameter. To achieve a round shape, flip the tortilla and rotate 180 degrees each time you press the tortilla with the rolling pin. Add a small sprinkle of flour for ease in rolling each time you turn or flip the dough. Stack the tortillas with pieces of waxed paper between them on a plate until all the dough is used. (My mother draped tortillas, edges slightly overlapping, around the rim of a large bowl, then covered them with a towel until ready to cook.)

Before cooking the tortillas, use a balled-up paper towel to apply a light coat of vegetable oil to the surface of the preheated *comal*.

Place a tortilla on the *comal*. Turn when a few bubbles appear on the surface, usually after about 30 seconds, depending on the *comal* and the stove burner, and cook the other side. Tortillas should have a few light brown spots on each side when thoroughly cooked.

Repeat the process with the remaining tortillas, oiling the *comal* as needed.

Place the tortillas in a tortilla warmer or in a bowl covered with a towel until they are all cooked.

Rolling flour tortillas

It is important to roll tortillas thin enough. They should be no thicker than the cover on a hardbound book. If too thick, flour tortillas will take longer to cook and won't produce bubbles to signal when it is time to turn them. Have patience with yourself while you get the hang of rolling round tortillas. You will soon acquire the touch, and your tortillas will be presentably round. Even my tortillas aren't always perfectly round, but they taste great!

Enchilada Queen Chicken Stock

This is one of my "core recipes." In the restaurants, we always have at least a five-gallon container of chicken stock ready for use that day and another potful simmering for tomorrow. We even use it to poach boneless chicken breasts to enrich the flavor. This stock is key to *Pollo Guisado* (page 45) and Chicken with *Salsa Suiza* (page 69) as well as many other recipes.　　　　**Makes 3 quarts**

1 (4-pound) whole chicken; or
　4 pounds bone-in, skin-on
　chicken parts
1½ cups chopped white onions
6 garlic cloves, peeled and
　smashed
3 bay leaves
2 stalks celery, coarsely
　chopped
1½ cups coarsely chopped
　tomatoes
¾ cup coarsely chopped carrots
2 teaspoons finely ground black
　pepper
4 teaspoons salt

In a large saucepan or stockpot over high heat, combine the chicken, 3½ quarts water, the onions, garlic, bay leaves, celery, tomatoes, carrots, pepper, and salt. Bring to a boil, then reduce heat and simmer for 1 hour.

Set aside off the heat to cool for about 30 minutes. Remove the chicken and let cool enough to handle. Remove and discard the skin and bones. Reserve cooked chicken for use in recipes.

Pour the broth through a fine strainer into a clean container. Discard the solids. Place the broth in the refrigerator until the fat congeals. Spoon the fat from the broth and discard. Refrigerate or freeze until ready to use in recipes.

Sylvia's Flavor Tricks

Salt is without doubt the most important component when it comes to seasoning. One very simple and valuable thing I learned in the product development labs at Uncle Ben's Rice is that salt is *the* critical ingredient in any formula or recipe.

All the recipes in this book use standard iodized table salt. Please remember to adjust measurements accordingly if using flaked or ground kosher salt as different types and brands measure differently.

In very simple terms, salt is a *flavor enhancer* in virtually every recipe, whether sweet or savory. Salt brings all spices and flavors to life with just one quick application. If all ingredients are in perfect proportions for a full-flavored result but the salt level is low, the flavor will be sleepy or unimpressive.

When I do a line check of the dishes before a shift and find a sauce, for example, that isn't quite right, the solution typically is to add more salt and all the flavors suddenly pop. Needless to say, I really focus on determining the best level of salt when I develop a recipe. And I always stress in my kitchens and cooking classes that salt should be measured accurately each and every time. The old throw-away line about tossing a "pinch" of salt into the recipe at the end of cooking does not work for me.

That's why I specify measurements, even of salt, in most of my recipes. Of course, you may want to adjust to your taste and health requirements, if you have special dietary needs. But be assured that I have made every effort to make sure that flavors in my recipes are vibrant and balanced.

Many recipes in this book call for a spice paste I call the Tex-Mex Holy Trinity. Just as Cajun cuisine relies on the Holy Trinity of chopped onions, celery, and green bell peppers; garlic, cumin, and black pepper form the flavor backbone of many recipes in border cooking. Many great *frontera* cooks prepare this combination in bulk so they don't have to grind the spices every time a recipe or dish calls for it.

This combination of garlic, cumin, and black pepper gives a distinctly border flavor. The emphasis on cumin is very Tex-Mex. While cumin is often used in Mexican cooking, it is always blended with all "the other" spices. In Tex-Mex cooking, cumin makes a bold aroma and flavor statement. For example, cumin is the characteristic aroma of *chili con carne*. Like the accordion in *cajunto* music, cumin comes through loud and clear.

For convenience, make a big or small batch of the Tex-Mex Holy Trinity (page 20) and store in the refrigerator up to a month. A couple of teaspoons is about the right amount for most recipes. And it will be at hand when you need it. Don't let grinding the Tex-Mex Holy Trinity slow you down. And don't reserve this blend exclusively for Enchilada Queen recipes. Experiment with the Tex-Mex Holy Trinity in almost any dish or savory cooking application.

The Tex-Mex Holy Trinity (Big Batch)
GARLIC, CUMIN, AND BLACK PEPPER SPICE PASTE

Makes 1 cup

Special Equipment

- Molcajete, mortar and pestle, or spice or coffee grinder

30 garlic cloves, peeled
6 tablespoons water, added 2 tablespoons at a time
⅓ cup cumin seeds
¼ cup whole black peppercorns

In a *molcajete*, mortar and pestle, or spice or coffee grinder, combine the garlic and 2 tablespoons water. Process until the garlic is a smooth paste. Remove garlic paste to a small bowl.

Repeat with the cumin seeds, then the peppercorns, adding 2 tablespoons water each time. Add the ground cumin and peppercorns to the small bowl.

Stir the garlic well with a rubber spatula. Store in an airtight container in the refrigerator for up to 1 month.

Use about 2 teaspoons in recipes calling for this trio of flavors or in any dish that will benefit from this flavor profile.

The Tex-Mex Holy Trinity (Small Batch)
GARLIC, CUMIN, AND BLACK PEPPER SPICE PASTE

Makes about 4 teaspoons

Special Equipment

- Molcajete, mortar and pestle, or spice or coffee grinder

3 garlic cloves, peeled
1½ teaspoons cumin seeds
1¼ teaspoons whole black peppercorns

Combine the garlic, cumin, peppercorns, and 1 tablespoon water in a *molcajete*, mortar and pestle, or spice or coffee grinder. Process until the garlic is a smooth paste and the spices are finely ground.

Transfer to a small container with a lid.

Store in the refrigerator for up to 1 month.

Opposite: The Holy Trinity spice blend in *molcajete* (mortar and pestle).
Ingredients, L to R, cumin, garlic, black pepper.

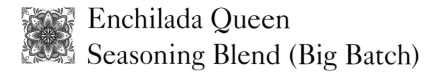

Enchilada Queen Seasoning Blend (Big Batch)

This is a seasoning blend I use for grilling. It is a good all-purpose combo that can go in the batter for fish tacos or be used as a seasoning for poultry, pork, beef, or lamb for any cooking method, including roasting.

Makes about 1 cup

¼ cup garlic powder

¼ cup onion powder

¼ cup freshly ground black pepper

6 teaspoons salt

¼ teaspoon cayenne pepper

Combine all the ingredients in a small container or shaker. Store in an airtight container in a dark place or refrigerate for up to 6 months.

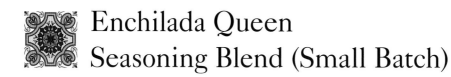

Enchilada Queen Seasoning Blend (Small Batch)

Makes about ⅓ cup

4 teaspoons garlic powder

4 teaspoons onion powder

4 teaspoons freshly ground black pepper

2 teaspoons salt

⅛ teaspoon cayenne pepper

Combine all the ingredients in a small container or shaker. Store in an airtight container in a dark place or refrigerate for up to 6 months.

Enchilada Queen Grilled Vegetable Seasoning Blend

Makes about 2 tablespoons

1½ teaspoons salt

2 teaspoons garlic powder

2 teaspoons onion powder

1 teaspoon smoked paprika

½ teaspoon cayenne pepper

½ teaspoon sugar

In a shaker or small bowl, blend all the ingredients together. Store in an airtight container in a dark place or refrigerate for up to 6 months.

Enchilada Queen Lime, Garlic, and White Wine Butter

Use this flavored butter to brush on shrimp or fish before grilling. It is also good on chicken and quail. Note that I use lime in this multipurpose sauce. That's because I grew up in an area where limes were the basic citrus for cooking. Along the border in heavily Mexican-influenced areas, lemons are considered *limones amarillo* (yellow limes).

Makes about 2 cups

1 cup (2 sticks) unsalted butter

Juice of ½ lime

2 tablespoons olive oil

6 garlic cloves, thinly sliced

2 tablespoons Worcestershire sauce

¾ cup dry white wine

In a medium saucepan over low heat, melt the butter. Add the lime juice and set aside off the heat.

In a medium skillet over low heat, combine the oil and garlic. Cook until the garlic is slightly browned and soft, about 5 minutes.

Add the garlic and oil, Worcestershire sauce, and wine to the butter mixture and bring to a boil. Lower the heat and simmer for about 5 minutes.

Set aside to cool for 30 minutes. Strain the sauce through a fine strainer; discard the solids.

To store, cover and refrigerate. Keeps 1 week.

If refrigerated, heat in a microwave oven briefly to liquefy. Brush on shrimp or fish before grilling.

Sylvia's Brine for Grilling

Marinating *cabrito*, pork, or quail in this intensely flavored brine before grilling makes for succulent meat or poultry. Brining helps meat and poultry retain juices during cooking. Depending upon the size of the *cabrito*, double the amount of water and salt to completely immerse the whole carcass, usually about 4 feet long and a couple of feet wide when split down the breast to butterfly it. For big pieces like a split *cabrito*, place the carcass in a large cooler with enough brine to cover. Keep cool by adding refreezable ice packs to the cooler and rotating in more frozen packs every 4 hours. You will need several ice packs: Remove, wash, and refreeze them.   **Makes 1½ quarts**

16 garlic cloves, smashed
2 cups coarsely chopped onions
2½ teaspoons salt

In a blender jar, combine the garlic and 1½ cups water. Process until smooth.

Add the onion and process again until smooth.

Transfer pureed onion and garlic to 1½-quart container with a tight-fighting lid.

Add the salt and 4½ cups water. Stir well to combine.

Pour enough brine over the chicken, quail, or *cabrito* (or other meat or poultry) to immerse and place in plastic bag or nonreactive container and cover tightly. Refrigerate for 4 hours or up to overnight.

One hour before grilling, pour off the brine and pat the meat or poultry dry. Allow the meat or poultry to come to room temperature.

CHAPTER 3

ENCHILADA QUEEN SAUCES

The Heart and Soul of Rio Grande Cuisine

The fourteen sauces in this chapter comprise the flavor base of most of my dishes, from enchiladas to grilled red snapper. My sauces represent the classic Mexican and Tex-Mex sauces used in Rio Grande cuisine, as well as some I've created over the years for my signature enchiladas.

South of the border, green, red, and chunky tomato sauces make up the three major sauce categories of Mexican cuisine. North of the border, chili gravy is the trademark of Tex-Mex.

Green sauces or *salsas verdes* are based on tomatillos, also known as Mexican husk tomatoes (see *Salsa Verde*, page 38). About the size of golf balls, tomatillos are distinguished by a papery husk that has to be removed before using in a recipe.

Red sauces or *salsas rojas* are made with dried red chiles, such as *Salsa Roja* (page 29), which are commonly used for white cheese (*queso fresco*) enchiladas in Mexico. I include *moles* in this category as most *mole* sauces use ground red chiles along with a wide variety of ingredients including chocolate, the distinguishing ingredient of many *moles*.

Salsa Veracruzana (page 36) represents the chunky tomato genre of Mexican sauces often used on grilled dishes, *a la parilla*, and seafood. My version of *Veracruzana*, very Mediterranean in style, includes red tomatoes, capers, and olives. I use it on shrimp enchiladas and grilled red snapper.

That brings us to Tex-Mex sauces, characterized by Chili Gravy (page 27). That's the reddish brown sauce that tops beef and yellow cheese enchiladas on typical Tex-Mex menus. This chapter also include sauces that I've created for enchiladas that go beyond the standards, such as *Salsa de Crema* (page 40) used on squash enchiladas (page 68).

Note that throughout this book you will see references to "chili gravy": spelled like *chili con carne*—that is, the American bowl of red chile beef stew often simply called chili, usually made with chili powder. You will also see references to "chile sauce," which means sauces made with dried and fresh chile peppers. I agree this can be somewhat confusing. But it is yet another example of the blending of cuisines to make Tex-Mex.

While I use my sauces in specific dishes in this book and the restaurants, please don't consider that a limitation. It should be inspiration. Use these delicious multitalented sauces any way you like. *Salsa Verde* doesn't have to be reserved for chicken enchiladas. Try it with pork or cheese enchiladas—or scrambled eggs.

To achieve the smooth texture desired in many of these sauces, ingredients are processed using a blender or food processor. Every day I (and my kitchen staff) thank heaven for modern tools with motors. Can you imagine using a *molcajete* or *metate* (stone mortars and pestles) to achieve that smooth texture? *That's* when cooking was work!

Few Mexican or Tex-Mex restaurants produce as many fresh sauces as we do at Sylvia's Enchilada Kitchen. The variety and culinary range of my sauces distinguish my restaurants. Through our sauces (those marked "v" are vegetarian), it is possible to taste your way through Rio Grande cuisine, with all its Mexican and Tex-Mex influences.

Classic Tex-Mex Chili Gravy

Chili gravy is *the* sauce for which my restaurants are known, the one we do better than most other Mexican restaurants. This is everybody's favorite—and the basic—Tex-Mex-style sauce for beef and yellow cheese enchiladas. It is called "chili" gravy, spelled with two i's, because it has beef and chili powder in it, à la Texas' *chili con carne*. In this version, the beef cooks down so much that it is hardly visible or palpable, but its presence on the palate is indisputable.

When working on this recipe, I kept in mind what veteran restaurateurs told me: "To be successful, every restaurant has to do one thing better than everyone else." For Sylvia's Enchilada Kitchen, our best is chili gravy.

Makes about 5 cups, enough for 10 to 12 enchiladas

1½ cups chopped white onions

5 garlic cloves, smashed

¼ cup ground beef, crumbled

⅔ cup vegetable oil

⅔ cup all-purpose flour

2 cups beef broth

3 tablespoons chili powder

2 teaspoons salt

2 teaspoons Tex-Mex Holy Trinity (page 20)

⅛ teaspoon cayenne pepper

Use for
Enchiladas Refugio (page 57),
Enchiladas El Paso (page 63),
Enchiladas McAllen (page 60),
Enchiladas Donna (page 59),
Enchiladas Kineña (page 61)

In a blender jar, combine the onions, garlic, and ½ cup water. Process on high speed for 1 minute, or until smooth.

In a small saucepan over low heat, combine the crumbled beef, 2 cups water, and the processed onion and garlic. Simmer, uncovered, for 30 minutes. Using a large spoon, skim the frothy substance that rises to the surface; discard. Repeat 2 or 3 times during the cooking time. Also use the spoon to break up clumps of meat for a smooth consistency. Set aside off the heat.

In a large skillet over medium heat, heat the oil until it shimmers. Lower the heat. Stirring continuously, add the flour and cook until the flour turns a light golden color. Set aside off the heat.

In a medium saucepan over low heat, heat the broth and 1 cup water until steaming hot, almost boiling. Meanwhile, in a small bowl or container with a lid, combine the chili powder, salt, Holy Trinity, and cayenne pepper, whisking or shaking to blend. Stir the combined spices into the hot broth mixture, blending until smooth.

Gradually add the cooked beef and chili powder–broth mixture to the cooked flour, stirring constantly to remove lumps. Stir and cook over low heat for 5 minutes, or until the mixture is almost as thick as ketchup.

Set aside off the heat for at least 10 minutes before serving.

The sauce may be refrigerated for up to 1 week or frozen for up to 3 months.

Chili con Carne Gravy

This is a version of *chili con carne*—the state dish of Texas—for which the state is justifiably famous. A great sauce for cheese enchiladas, *chili con carne* gravy can, of course, be eaten as chili stew, aka "a bowl of red." At home, we always called it "gravy" to distinguish it from more traditional Mexican styles of sauce. This Tex-Mex vernacular is similar to the Italian-American reference to "Sunday gravy," a meaty red sauce for pasta.

Makes about 5 cups, enough for 10 to 12 enchiladas

1½ cups chopped white onions

4 garlic cloves, smashed

1 pound ground beef

¼ cup vegetable oil

¼ cup all-purpose flour

2 cups beef broth

2 teaspoons Tex-Mex Holy Trinity (page 20)

¼ cup chili powder

1 teaspoon salt

In blender jar, combine onion and garlic and process on high for about 1 minute or until it is a smooth consistency.

In a medium saucepan over medium heat, cook the beef until brown, stirring frequently. Drain off the fat.

To the saucepan, add ¼ cup water and the processed onion and garlic. Simmer for 15 minutes. Set aside off the heat.

In a large, deep skillet or saucepan over medium heat, heat the oil until it shimmers. Lower the heat and whisk in the flour. Cook, stirring continuously, until the flour turns light tan in color to make a light roux. Set aside off the heat.

In a small saucepan or a microwave-safe measuring cup, combine the broth and ¼ cup water. Heat to boiling. Keep warm.

Combine the Holy Trinity, chili powder, and salt in a small bowl or container. Mix well.

Return the large skillet or saucepan with the cooked flour to low heat. Gradually add the spice mixture, hot broth, and beef mixture to the flour, stirring until smooth. Cook over low heat for 5 minutes, or until the mixture thickens slightly.

Set aside off the heat for at least 10 minutes to let the flavors mellow before serving.

The sauce may be refrigerated up to 1 week or frozen for up to 3 months.

Salsa Roja ⓥ

This particular sauce is the most bicultural of all. In Mexico, *Salsa Roja* is the traditional sauce for enchiladas filled with white cheese (*queso fresco*). It is also very popular for stacked enchiladas à la El Paso. *Salsa Roja* has a smoky, dried chile flavor. A touch of *chiles de arbol* gives it the right amount of heat.

This sauce is very similar to New Mexico red chile sauce that typically uses dried poblano peppers, called ancho chiles in their desiccated form. The *chile guajillo* is a dried mirasol pepper.

Makes about 5 cups, enough for 10 to 12 enchiladas

12 guajillo chiles, stems and
   seeds removed
3 *chiles de arbol*, stems removed
   (no need to remove seeds)
2 tablespoons vegetable oil
½ white onion, chopped
3 garlic cloves, finely chopped
1½ teaspoons salt

Use for
Enchiladas Morelia (page 72),
Enchiladas El Paso (page 63)

In a small saucepan over high heat, combine the dried chiles and 2½ cups water. Bring to a boil, reduce the heat, and simmer for 15 minutes.

Set aside off the heat for 10 minutes to cool.

In a blender jar or food processor work bowl, process the chiles and their cooking liquid 1 minute, or until smooth.

Pour the pureed chile mixture through a fine strainer into a small bowl, pressing with the back of a spoon to extract as much liquid and smooth pulp as possible; set aside. Discard the solids.

In a medium skillet over medium heat, heat the oil until it shimmers. Add the onion and cook until soft and translucent, 3 to 5 minutes. Stir in the garlic, cooking just until the garlic is golden.

Add 1½ cups water, the chile puree, and salt; simmer for about 15 minutes.

Set aside off the heat for at least 10 minutes to let the flavors mellow before serving.

The sauce may be refrigerated up to 1 week or frozen for up to 3 months.

Salsa Hidalgo Roja ✔

Salsa Hidalgo Roja is the hottest of the tomato and chile enchilada sauces I make. It uses very spicy varieties of peppers, either *chiles de arbol* or *de pequin*, in addition to jalapeño. They are small but mighty, in terms of heat. Remember to use food handlers' gloves when working with dried or fresh chiles, especially these extremely hot ones.

Makes about 4 cups, enough for 8 to 10 enchiladas

5 tomatoes (about 2 pounds), coarsely chopped
½ white onion, chopped
½ jalapeño, cut into 4 pieces
3 garlic cloves, finely chopped
1½ teaspoons salt
10 *chiles de arbol*, or 5 *chiles de pequin*
¼ cup finely chopped fresh cilantro leaves

Use for
Enchiladas Hidalgo Roja
(page 81)

Preheat the oven to 350°F.

In a medium saucepan over high heat, combine the tomatoes, onion, jalapeño, garlic, salt, and 1½ cups water. Bring to a boil. Reduce the heat and simmer for about 20 minutes. Set aside off the heat to cool for about 10 minutes.

While the tomatoes are cooling, place the dried chiles in a single layer on a baking sheet and roast in the oven for 3 to 4 minutes, until the edges are brown and the skin begins to peel.

In a blender jar or work bowl of a food processor, combine the tomato mixture, the roasted chiles, and the cilantro. Process on low speed for about 15 seconds, then on high for another 15 to 20 seconds or until all the chiles are liquefied and smooth.

Transfer the sauce to a medium saucepan and place over medium heat until heated through. Set aside off the heat for at least 10 minutes to let the flavors mellow before serving.

The sauce may be refrigerated up to 1 week or frozen for up to 3 months.

Salsa Ranchera ⓥ

Made with fresh jalapeños, this sauce has vibrant flavor and color, assuming you can find fresh, vine-ripened tomatoes to complement the chiles. Use hot-house tomatoes if other tomatoes aren't ripe enough. This is a great sauce to make in the summer using tomatoes and peppers from your garden—or a neighbor's. Remember to use plastic food handlers' gloves when handling fresh jalapeños or other hot chile peppers to protect your hands, eyes, nose, and lips. Be careful not to touch your face with gloved hands that have handled fresh jalapeños, or you'll learn that lesson the hard way. Remove the jalapeño seeds if a milder sauce is desired.

Makes about 4 cups, enough for 8 to 10 enchiladas

7 tomatoes (about 3 pounds total), each cut into 4 pieces

3 fresh jalapeños, stems removed and seeds removed if desired, each cut into 4 pieces

2 tablespoons vegetable oil

½ large onion, cut into thin slices about 2 inches long

2 teaspoons Tex-Mex Holy Trinity (page 20)

1½ teaspoons salt

Use for
Enchiladas Chihuahua (page 77), *Huevos Rancheros* (page 150)

In a medium saucepan over high heat, combine the tomatoes and jalapeños with 2½ cups water. Bring to a boil, then reduce the heat and simmer for 20 minutes. Set aside off the heat to cool slightly.

In a blender jar or work bowl of a food processor, process the cooked tomatoes and jalapeños with their cooking liquid until smooth. Set aside.

In a large skillet over medium heat, heat the oil until it shimmers. Add the onion and cook until almost tender, 3 to 4 minutes. Add the Holy Trinity and cook until the garlic is soft, but not brown.

Add the tomato puree to the onion mixture, add the salt, and simmer over low heat for 8 to 10 minutes. Set aside off the heat for at least 10 minutes to let the flavors mellow before serving. Reheat gently, if needed, on the stovetop or in a microwave oven on low power until heated through.

The sauce may be refrigerated for up to 1 week or frozen for up to 3 months.

Mole Puebla or Poblano

This is real deal *mole.* I use it on several dishes in my restaurants. Using homemade chicken stock (page 18) yields the deepest flavor, although in a pinch, canned or packaged broth will do. For an extra flavor boost, I add some instant chicken bouillon. I prefer the Knorr brand favored in Mexican and Mexican-American kitchens.

I also rely on another name brand cherished in Mexico and along the Rio Grande, Nestlé Abuelita chocolate. Ibarra is another popular brand in Mexico. Found in Mexican groceries and supermarkets or the Mexican food section of many supermarkets in the Southwest, Abuelita chocolate gives this *mole* its chocolate character. Dried chiles give it punch and soul. If Abuelita or Ibarra brands aren't available, substitute top-quality semisweet chocolate, such as Ghirardelli Semi-Sweet Baking Bar, Callebaut semisweet chocolate block, or Baker's Semi-Sweet Baking Chocolate Bar.

Yet another favorite border product, Gamesa-brand *María galletas* (tea biscuit cookies), are used to give body and richness to this sauce.

Makes about 4 cups, enough for 10 to 12 enchiladas

4 pasilla chiles, stems and seeds removed

4 guajillo chiles, stems and seeds removed

2 ancho chiles, stems and seeds removed

15 *María galletas* (Gamesa brand preferred)

3 cups chicken stock (page 18)

3 Abuelita chocolate tablets, or 3 ounces semisweet chocolate, broken into small pieces

5 teaspoons peanut butter

½ cup chopped white onion

2 garlic cloves, smashed

¼ cup vegetable oil

1 tablespoon chicken base or Knorr chicken bouillon

(continued)

In a medium saucepan over low heat, combine the chiles and 2½ cups water. Bring to a boil, then lower the heat and simmer for 15 minutes. Set aside off the heat to cool for 15 minutes.

In a blender jar or food processor work bowl, process the chiles and their cooking liquid for 1 minute, or until smooth and the chiles are liquefied.

Pour the pureed chile mixture through a fine strainer into a small bowl, pressing with the back of a spoon to extract as much liquid and smooth pulp as possible; set aside. Discard the solids.

In the work bowl of a food processer, process 8 of the cookies to fine crumbs. Repeat with the remaining cookies. Set the crumbs aside.

In a small saucepan over low heat, warm the chicken broth. Add the chocolate tablets, one at a time, stirring constantly, until melted and blended to a smooth consistency. Set aside off the heat.

1 teaspoon sugar

1 teaspoon salt

⅛ teaspoon ground cumin

⅛ teaspoon freshly ground
  black pepper

½ to ¾ teaspoons cayenne
  pepper, or to taste

Use for
Enchiladas Puebla (page 78)

In a blender jar, process the peanut butter, onion, and garlic for a few seconds to combine. Add the cookie crumbs and chocolate liquid. Process until smooth, about 1 minute.

Pour the peanut butter–chocolate mixture through a fine strainer into a small bowl, pressing with the back of a spoon to extract as much liquid as possible; set aside. Discard the solids.

In a large deep skillet or saucepan over high heat, warm the oil. Add the strained chile puree. Lower the heat and simmer, stirring frequently, for about 10 minutes.

Using a whisk, blend in the chocolate–peanut butter–cookie crumb mixture, the chicken base, sugar, salt, cumin, and black pepper. Add cayenne as desired, ½ teaspoon at a time.

Over low heat, simmer for 10 minutes, or until the sauce is the consistency of ketchup. Reheat gently, if needed, on the stovetop or in a microwave oven on low power until heated through.

The sauce may be refrigerated for up to 1 week or frozen for up to 3 months.

Salsa Casera ⓥ

This is a mild, marinara-style sauce spiced with fresh serrano chile, onion, and garlic. It is a mellow blend that goes well with stewed chicken for a classic Mexican-style chicken enchilada. It's quick and very simple to prepare and is often a fall-back for Rio Grande home cooks as a last-minute meal preparation.   *Makes about 4 cups, enough for 8 to 10 enchiladas*

5 tomatoes (about 2 pounds), coarsely chopped

½ fresh serrano chile, cut in half lengthwise and seeded

½ yellow onion, peeled and thinly sliced into 1-inch-long strips

1½ teaspoons salt

¼ teaspoon freshly ground black pepper

5 garlic cloves, minced

In a large saucepan over high heat, combine the tomatoes, chile, onion, 1¼ cups water, the salt, and pepper. Bring to a boil, then reduce the heat and simmer for about 20 minutes. Set aside off the heat to cool for about 10 minutes.

Add the garlic and mash the cooked mixture with a potato masher until the tomatoes and serrano are slightly chunky.

Set aside for at least 10 minutes to let the flavors mellow before serving.

The sauce may be refrigerated for up to 1 week or frozen for up to 3 months.

Use for
**Enchiladas Guadalajara
(page 82)**

Salsa Española ⓥ

Salsa Española is a "no heat" recipe. The flavor profile reflects Spanish influence, as it is made with olive oil and without chiles. In fact, it has a little sugar, which sets it apart from any other Mexican-style sauce. It is a favorite in many homes in South Texas. In addition to enchiladas, *Salsa Española* makes a good accompaniment to any vegetarian dish.

Makes about 4 cups, enough for 8 to 10 enchiladas

10 Roma tomatoes, seeded and cut into 4 pieces
2 tablespoons olive oil
1 white onion, peeled and thinly sliced into 1-inch-long strips
3 garlic cloves, minced
⅓ cup chopped celery
½ cup chopped bell pepper
1 teaspoon salt
1 teaspoon sugar
½ teaspoon freshly ground black pepper

Use for
Enchiladas Monterrey (page 76)

In a medium saucepan over high heat, combine the tomatoes and 1½ cups water; bring to a boil. Cover, lower the heat, and simmer for 15 minutes. Uncover and set aside off the heat for about 10 minutes.

In a blender jar or work bowl of a food processor, process the tomatoes and their liquid until very smooth. Set aside.

In a 10-inch skillet over medium heat, heat the oil until it shimmers. Add the onion and garlic; cook until the onion is soft and translucent, about 3 minutes.

To the skillet, add the blended tomatoes, the celery, bell pepper, salt, sugar, and black pepper. Lower the heat and simmer for 15 minutes, stirring occasionally.

Set aside off the heat for at least 10 minutes to let the flavors mellow before serving.

The sauce may be refrigerated for up to 1 week or frozen for up to 3 months.

Salsa Veracruzana ⓥ

This chunky tomato sauce, with distinct Mediterranean flavors including capers, is of the style used for seafood dishes in Mexico. I like it on shrimp enchiladas and grilled fish.

Makes about 4 cups, enough for 8 to 10 enchiladas

¼ cup virgin olive oil
1 cup chopped white onion
2 garlic cloves, minced
1 jalapeño, seeded and minced
5 large Roma tomatoes, coarsely chopped
¼ cup tomato sauce
2 tablespoons sliced green olives with pimientos
1 bay leaf
⅛ teaspoon ground cumin
⅛ teaspoon freshly ground black pepper
½ teaspoon salt
½ teaspoon distilled white vinegar
2 tablespoons drained capers

In a medium skillet over medium heat, heat the oil until it shimmers. Add the onion, garlic, and jalapeño. Stir and cook until the onion is translucent and begins to soften, about 3 minutes.

Add the tomatoes, tomato sauce, olives, bay leaf, cumin, black pepper, salt, and vinegar. Bring to a boil over high heat. Lower the heat and simmer for 20 minutes.

Add the capers. Set aside off the heat for at least 10 minutes to let the flavors mellow before serving.

The sauce may be refrigerated for up to 1 week or frozen for up to 3 months.

Use for
**Enchiladas Tampico (page 75),
Grilled Red Snapper (page 113)**

Salsa Suiza ⓥ

This sauce has a creamy element with the addition of Mexican *crema*. Widely available in the Southwest and western states, *crema* is thinner than sour cream, pourable, and has a tang. Crème fraîche is the best widely available substitute. Mild, yet with an excellent acid balance from the tomatillos, this pale green sauce is like tomatillo velvet.

Makes about 4 cups, enough for 8 to 10 enchiladas

1½ pounds tomatillos, rinsed after peeling papery outer skin, cut in half
1 tomato, cut into 4 pieces
½ white onion, chopped
2 garlic cloves, minced
½ cup Mexican *crema* or crème fraîche
1 teaspoon salt

Use for
Enchiladas San Miguel (page 69)

In a medium saucepan over high heat, combine the tomatillos, tomato, onion, garlic, and 2½ cups water. Bring to a boil, then reduce the heat and simmer for about 20 minutes. Set aside off the heat for 10 minutes to cool.

In a blender jar or work bowl of a food processor, process the tomatillo mixture for 1 minute, or until smooth.

Pour the processed tomatillo mixture through a fine strainer into a saucepan, pressing with the back of a spoon to extract as much liquid and smooth pulp as possible; set aside. Discard the solids.

Place the saucepan with the blended mixture over high heat. When the mixture bubbles, reduce the heat to medium. Off the boil, add the *crema* and salt. Simmer for 5 minutes.

Cover and keep warm to serve.

The sauce may be refrigerated for up to 3 days. Do not freeze.

Salsa Verde ⓥ

In Mexico, this is the iconic sauce for chicken enchiladas, and the sauce I use for spinach enchiladas as well. I also use it on *chilaquiles* (page 146), pan-fried tortilla pieces with green sauce. Last-minute additions of cilantro and garlic give this sauce a distinct flavor, and customers rave about it. It is my second best seller after chili gravy. *Salsa Verde* is as popular in South Texas as it is in Mexico.

Makes about 4 cups, enough for 8 to 10 enchiladas

1½ pounds tomatillos, rinsed after peeling papery outer skin, cut in half

½ large white onion, chopped

½ jalapeño, cut into 4 pieces (do not remove seeds)

1 large tomato, cut into 4 pieces

3 garlic cloves, minced

Leaves from ½ bunch fresh cilantro

1¼ teaspoons salt

Use for
Enchiladas Mexico City (page 71),
Enchiladas Crystal City (page 65)

In a large saucepan over medium heat, combine the tomatillos, onion, jalapeño, tomato, and 2½ cups water. Bring to a boil, then lower the heat and simmer for 20 minutes, or until all the ingredients are very soft. Set aside off the heat to cool for about 10 minutes.

In a blender jar or work bowl of a food processor, process the garlic, cilantro, and salt until smooth.

Add the tomatillo mixture. Process on high speed until very smooth, about 1 minute.

Set aside for at least 10 minutes to let the flavors mellow before serving. Reheat gently, if needed, on the stovetop or in a microwave oven on low power until heated through.

The sauce may be refrigerated for up to 1 week or frozen for up to 3 months.

Salsa de Crema Verde ❤

A first cousin to *Salsa Verde*, this delicious green sauce is more complex. I use it with pork *carnitas*. The creamy character derives from a touch of sour cream and avocado; it could also be a very rich, piquant soup. **Makes about 4 cups, enough for 8 to 10 enchiladas**

1½ pounds tomatillos, rinsed after peeling papery outer skin, cut in half

1 tomato, coarsely chopped

1 white onion, chopped

½ jalapeño, seeded and cut into 4 pieces

1¼ teaspoons salt

Leaves from ⅓ bunch fresh cilantro

2 garlic cloves, smashed

1 avocado, coarsely chopped

2 tablespoons sour cream

Use for
Enchiladas Hidalgo Verde
(page 80).

In a large saucepan over high heat, combine the tomatillos, tomato, onion, jalapeño, salt, and 1 cup water. Bring to a boil, then lower the heat and simmer for 20 minutes, or until the tomatillos are very soft. Set aside off the heat for 10 minutes.

In a blender jar or work bowl of a food processor, process the tomatillo mixture in two batches until smooth. Set aside in a clean saucepan.

In the blender jar or work bowl of the food processor, combine the cilantro, garlic, avocado, and sour cream. Process until smooth. Add to the saucepan, stirring well to combine.

Set aside for at least 10 minutes to let the flavors mellow before serving. Reheat gently, if needed, on the stovetop or in a microwave oven on low power until heated through. Do not boil.

The sauce may be refrigerated for up to 3 days. Do not freeze.

Salsa de Crema

This sauce may be a surprise if you think of Tex-Mex as only about chili gravy. This delicate cream sauce could as easily cover crêpes as tortillas. The subtle flavors combine with the down-to-earth taste and texture of corn tortillas to make very sophisticated and enticing enchilada combinations. It is my creation for enchiladas filled with *calabacitas*, Mexican squash. I rinse and drain the tomatoes in a coarse colander to remove the seeds and juices so as not to dilute the sauce.

Makes about 4 cups, enough for 8 to 10 enchiladas

1 cup milk

1 cup heavy whipping cream

1 cup chicken broth (page 18)

½ cup (1 stick) unsalted butter

½ cup all-purpose flour

2 tablespoons vegetable oil

½ cup diced white onion

2 garlic cloves, minced

½ cup diced tomato, seeded, rinsed, and drained

½ cup chopped fresh cilantro leaves

1 teaspoon salt

Use for
Enchiladas Sarita (page 68)

In a medium saucepan over medium heat, combine the milk, cream, and broth. Heat until very warm but not boiling. Set aside off the heat.

In a large skillet over low heat, melt the butter, stirring gently. Stir in the flour and cook until the mixture bubbles and turns golden.

Stirring constantly with a whisk, slowly add the warm milk mixture to the butter and flour. Cook and stir over low heat until smooth and thickened, about 5 minutes. Set aside off the heat.

In a small skillet over medium heat, combine the oil, onion, and garlic. Stir and cook until the onion is soft but not browned. Add the cooked onion to the sauce and cook over low heat for about 5 minutes. Do not boil.

Stir in the tomato, cilantro, and salt; simmer for another 5 minutes. Do not boil.

Set aside off the heat for at least 10 minutes to let the flavors mellow before serving.

The sauce may be refrigerated for up to 3 days. Do not freeze.

Salsa de Jaiba

This sauce is a variation of *Salsa de Crema* (page 40) with a spectacular addition: fresh crabmeat. I, of course, prefer blue crab from the Gulf of Mexico. This could also be served as cream of crab soup. When customers try my *Salsa de Jaiba*, they fall in love.

Makes about 4¼ cups, enough for 8 to 10 enchiladas

2 to 3 *chiles de arbol,* stems and
   seeds removed
1 tablespoon tomato sauce
1 recipe (4 cups) *Salsa de Crema*
   (page 40), heated through
¼ to ½ cup lump crabmeat

Use for
**Enchiladas Laguna Madre
(page 66)**

Using a *molcajete*, mortar and pestle, or spice or coffee grinder, grind the dried chiles with about 1 tablespoon water to make a smooth paste without visible chile skins.

Add the chile paste and tomato sauce to warm *Salsa de Crema* over low heat. Simmer for about 5 minutes. Stir in the crabmeat and simmer for 3 to 5 minutes longer for the crab to absorb flavor.

CHAPTER 4

ENCHILADA QUEEN WISDOM

or Why Sylvia Is "the Queen"

Enchiladas are the comfort food of Mexico. They're a comfort staple in Tex-Mex cuisine as well. And they're in the backbone of my beloved Rio Grande cuisine, which draws from both.

More than tacos, tamales, or *mole*, enchiladas are the national dish of Mexico. Enchiladas reflect Mexico's history, agriculture, and traditions. Enchiladas are the ultimate *campesino* (Mexican peasant) dish gone mainstream, even gourmet. Enchiladas are also the emblematic dish of Tex-Mex.

No Mexican and few Rio Grande family celebrations are complete without enchiladas. Beloved in home cooking and in restaurants, enchiladas' universal appeal makes them central to my subject: Rio Grande cuisine, a true blending of culinary cultures.

There are as many versions of enchiladas as there are cooks who make them, regardless of whether the kitchens are in Mexico, Texas, or anywhere. Though there are differences in fillings, sauces, and cheeses, there is one constant: Enchiladas are made with thin corn tortillas.

In Mexico, fillings are usually chicken, pork, white cheese, or seafood. Mexican enchiladas are often garnished with lettuce, tomato, grated or sliced radishes, sour cream, and *queso fresco*, a crumbly white Mexican cheese. Enchiladas in Mexico are not as heavily sauced as Tex-Mex iterations, and Mexican sauces are usually milder, not as hot and spicy.

Yellow cheese fillings and grated yellow cheese garnishes are distinguishing characteristics of Tex-Mex. In addition, typical Tex-Mex enchilada fillings include ground beef or taco meat, chicken, and fajita meat. Chili gravy is another strictly Tex-Mex touch. Tex-Mex garnishes are usually limited to grated yellow cheese. And lots of Tex-Mex lovers ask for finely chopped onions scattered on top of their cheese enchiladas swathed with chili gravy.

At Sylvia's Enchilada Kitchen, I serve both north- and south-of-the-border enchiladas and love them equally. Besides Mexican and Tex-Mex enchilada dishes, my restaurant menu offers several enchiladas I developed to satisfy vegetarians and seafood lovers. Since I created them, I claim them as part of my own style of Rio Grande cuisine.

The universal popularity of enchiladas is why I focus on them in my restaurants.

Another reason is because enchiladas often don't get enough respect, at least in some Tex-Mex joints. In too many Tex-Mex restaurants, enchiladas are an afterthought and unimaginatively filled with bland taco meat, shredded chicken, or tasteless processed yellow cheese; smothered in greasy chili gravy; then subjected to hours under heat lamps or on warming trays. The tortillas either dry out or disintegrate, depending on how much gloppy sauce has been applied.

The recipes in this book use less sauce than many typical enchilada recipes. In the restaurants, each plate of enchiladas is made to order. For the book, enchiladas are assembled, sauced and heated in casserole dishes. Please note that the directions call for leaving a small space between enchiladas. Do this. It is easier to remove the enchiladas from the pan and each enchilada is distinct, not a gloppy mess.

Because I grew up eating Mexican as well as Tex-Mex enchiladas made with love and care, I know enchiladas can be so much more. That's one reason my enchiladas are so popular: I cook enchiladas—and everything—with TLC (tender loving care), and fresh ingredients. I also take the time to do it right.

The recipes in this book reflect my preferences for enchiladas, what I serve my customers, friends, and family, whether I make enchiladas in my restaurant kitchens or my home. In that sense, this book makes no effort to be comprehensive and offer exhaustive examples of every enchilada genre. Instead, these recipes reflect my favorite versions and what I feel are the best examples of Mexican and Tex-Mex enchiladas, expressed as Rio Grande cuisine.

Making enchiladas is a multistep process finished as an assembly. It can also be a mix-and-match exercise, wherein you select your favorite sauce and filling, my combinations be damned. Of course you can do it all at once: Make the sauce, make the filling, flavor the tortillas using my Texas Two-Step technique (page 52), assemble, and bake. Or you can break up the steps: Make the sauce and filling a day or so ahead, refrigerate, and reheat to assemble and bake. Flavor the tortillas and let rest overnight if possible as well.

The way I make enchiladas isn't the fastest or the easiest. But it is *the best*!

About Monterey Jack cheese

Many recipes in this book call for Monterey Jack cheese. That is the marketing name of a white cheese made and sold commercially in California beginning in the mid-1800s. There are various stories about the name. Some versions have it that it was first known as "jack cheese" because it was made using a vise called a house jack to press the cheese. There is no doubt that businessman David Jacks popularized the cheese, first marketed as "jack cheese" and eventually Monterey Jack because Jacks exported it on ships out of the port of Monterey.

The origins of the cheese, known as *queso del pais* (country cheese), have been traced back to Franciscan monks in eighteenth-century Spain.

Fillings for Enchiladas

What goes into an enchilada is as important as the sauce. Flabby or flavorless fillings make enchiladas wimpy. Ground beef may be cooked with little or no seasoning and thrown into an enchilada. Ditto for chicken, boiled without seasoning and bland. Lot of restaurants use flavorless processed cheese because it melts so easily. I prefer the stronger flavor of real cheddar. Enchiladas filled with natural cheese must be baked for the cheese to melt. My fillings are carefully developed to impart great flavor to complement the sauce and the flavor of the spiced Texas Two-Step corn tortilla (page 54).

 # Rio Grande Ground Beef

This is the ground beef I use for beef enchiladas, Tex-Mex style. It can also be used to top nachos or to fill tacos. In a lot of homes, this was also a skillet dinner with sautéed, cubed potatoes or pasta to make the meat go further.

Makes about 3 cups

2 guajillo chiles, stems and seeds removed

2 *chiles de arbol*, stems removed (no need to remove seeds)

1½ pounds lean (90-10) ground beef, crumbled

2 teaspoons Tex-Mex Holy Trinity (page 20)

½ cup diced onion

½ cup diced tomato

1 teaspoon salt

Use for
Enchiladas Donna (page 59),
Tacos (page 101),
Nachos (page 96),
add to *Chile con Queso* (page 95)

In a medium saucepan over high heat, combine the chiles and 1¼ cups water. Bring to a boil, then reduce the heat and simmer for 10 minutes. Set aside off the heat for 10 minutes to cool.

In a blender jar or work bowl of a food processor, process the cooked chiles and all the liquid for 1 minute, or until smooth.

Pass the chile liquid through a fine strainer into a bowl; set aside. Discard the solids.

In a large skillet over medium heat, cook the beef, stirring frequently, for 4 to 5 minutes, until brown. Drain off the fat.

In a medium saucepan over low heat, combine 1 cup water, the strained chile puree, the Holy Trinity, onion, tomato, and salt. Cover and simmer for about 20 minutes.

Use a slotted spoon to scoop the meat from the cooking liquid, allowing each spoonful to drain before filling enchiladas.

Pollo Guisado
STEWED CHICKEN

Chicken, freshly cooked with spices and vegetables, reminds me of the old-fashioned flavor of our mother's cooking and the aroma of her kitchen. It is a staple of most border kitchens. This recipe for stewed chicken is very versatile. Besides enchiladas, it can be used to fill tamales and tacos.

Makes about 4 cups

1 (3-pound) chicken, whole or cut into 8 or 10 serving pieces
3½ teaspoons salt
2 teaspoons Tex-Mex Holy Trinity (page 20)
1 onion, chopped
2 bay leaves
1 large tomato, chopped
½ cup tomato sauce

Use for
Enchiladas McAllen (page 60),
Enchiladas Mexico City (page 71),
Enchiladas San Miguel (page 69),
Enchiladas Puebla (page 78),
Enchiladas Chihuahua (page 77),
Enchiladas Guadalajara (page 82),
Chicken Tamales (page 156),
Tacos (page 101)

In a large saucepan over high heat, combine the whole chicken or chicken pieces, 1 quart water, and 2 teaspoons of the salt. Bring to a boil, then reduce the heat and simmer, uncovered, for about 35 minutes.

Remove the chicken from the saucepan and allow to cool for about 30 minutes. Reserve the broth in a saucepan off the heat.

To the broth in the saucepan, add the Holy Trinity, the remaining 1½ teaspoons salt, the onion, bay leaves, tomato, and tomato sauce. Stir to combine.

When the chicken is cool enough to handle, remove the skin. Pull meat from the bones and shred the meat by hand or chop into bite-size pieces. Discard the skin and bones.

Over low heat, add the chicken to the broth mixture. Simmer for 20 minutes, or until soft.

Set aside off the heat for about 15 minutes to cool. Using a slotted spoon, transfer seasoned chicken meat to a clean container, draining most of the liquid.

Stewed Chicken Breast

Some of my customers prefer stewed chicken breast to *Pollo Guisado*, shredded light and dark meat from a whole chicken. This recipe produces chicken that is almost as moist and just as flavorful. It works particularly well with San Miguel and Puebla enchiladas. **Makes 4 cups**

2 pounds skin-on, bone-in chicken
  breasts
4 cups chicken stock (page 18)
1½ teaspoons salt
1 teaspoon garlic powder
1 teaspoon onion powder
1½ teaspoons freshly ground black
  pepper

Use for
Enchiladas San Miguel (page 69),
Enchiladas Puebla (page 78),
Tacos (page 101)

In a medium saucepan over high heat, combine the chicken, broth, and 1 teaspoon of the salt. Bring to a boil, then reduce the heat and simmer, uncovered, for about 25 minutes.

Using a slotted spoon, remove the chicken pieces from the cooking liquid and let cool. Set the cooking liquid aside off the heat.

When the chicken is cool enough to handle, remove the skin and any bones; discard. Cut the chicken meat into small bite-size pieces or shred by hand.

To the broth in the saucepan, add the chopped chicken, the garlic and onion powders, the remaining ½ teaspoon salt, and the pepper. Simmer for about 10 minutes over low heat, stirring occasionally.

Using a slotted spoon, transfer the seasoned chicken meat to a clean container, draining most of the liquid.

Carnitas
SLOW-FRIED PORK

Pigs are God's food gift to the poor. Edible from snout to tail, this wonderful, economical animal produces so many good things, especially delicious crispy pieces of pork called *carnitas*. I use *carnitas* for enchiladas with *roja* and *verde* sauces. Although unconventional, I also top *carnitas* enchiladas with *mole* sauce. Try some!

This recipe slow fries—that is, boils—a pork butt in oil, sort of like frying a turkey. The result is juicy meat with crispy ends. So delicious!

Makes about 2 cups

2 quarts vegetable oil

2 pounds boneless pork butt, in one piece

½ white onion, cut into 2 pieces

3 garlic cloves, smashed

1 teaspoon salt

1 teaspoon freshly ground black pepper

1 teaspoon dried thyme

1 (4-inch) cinnamon stick

Juice of 1 orange, squeezed halves reserved

Use for
Enchiladas Hidalgo Roja (page 81), Enchiladas Hidalgo Verde (page 80)

Put the oil in a 4-quart heavy stockpot and heat to 350°F. While the oil heats, trim any excess fat from the pork.

When the oil is hot, use a large slotted spoon to carefully lower the pork into the oil. Do not splash the hot oil.

Add the onion, garlic, salt, pepper, thyme, and cinnamon stick. Reduce the heat and cook at 212°F for 30 minutes.

After 30 minutes, add the orange juice and squeezed orange halves. Cook for 30 minutes longer at 212°F.

Remove from the heat and let the pork stand in the hot oil for about 15 minutes longer.

Using a slotted spoon, carefully remove the pork from the oil and set aside to cool. Discard the onion, garlic, cinnamon, and orange. After the oil cools completely, pour back into the original container and discard.

When the pork is cool enough to handle, cut into ½- to ¼-inch cubes.

Calabacitas and *Maiz* ❶

SQUASH AND CORN

Enchiladas filled with a combination of squash, corn, and tomato are among the most popular at my restaurants. *Calabacitas* are small green squash, similar in appearance to zucchini but a lighter green, widely available in Mexican markets. Zucchini can be substituted if true *calabacitas* aren't available. This vegetable dish is typically served as a skillet dinner with meat, not as an enchilada filling. I adapted it for a meatless enchilada.

Makes about 3 cups

2 tablespoons vegetable oil

½ onion, chopped

1 tomato, coarsely chopped

3 garlic cloves, minced

5 *calabacitas* (small green Mexican squash) or zucchini, cut into small pieces

Fresh corn cut from 2 cobs to make 1 cup, or 1 cup frozen whole kernel corn

½ cup tomato sauce

1½ cups chicken stock (page 18) or vegetable stock

2 teaspoons Tex-Mex Holy Trinity (page 20)

½ teaspoon salt

In a large skillet over medium heat, heat the oil until it shimmers. Add the onion, tomato, and garlic. Cook until the onion is soft and translucent but not browned, about 3 minutes.

Add the *calabacitas*, corn, tomato sauce, broth, Holy Trinity, and salt.

Cook over medium heat for about 10 minutes, until the *calabacitas* are tender.

Drain in a colander so that vegetable filling won't be runny.

Use for
Enchiladas Sarita (page 68)

Spinach ⓥ

This meatless filling is what I use for my popular Crystal City enchiladas, named after the small South Texas town that proclaims itself the spinach-growing capital of the universe. Going meatless? This vegetable filling will make your taste buds happy. *Makes 2 cups*

2 tablespoons vegetable oil
½ cup chopped onion
½ cup chopped bell pepper
2 garlic cloves, minced
1 teaspoon salt
2 (11-ounce) bags fresh spinach

Use for
Enchiladas Crystal City (page 65)

In a large skillet with a lid over medium heat, heat the oil until it shimmers. Add the onion, bell pepper, and garlic. Cook until the onion is soft and translucent but not browned, about 3 minutes.

Add ¼ cup water, the salt, and spinach. Cover and lower the heat. After 2 to 3 minutes, check to see if the spinach has wilted. When the spinach wilts, remove the lid and simmer over very low heat for 4 to 6 minutes. Drain excess liquid.

Shrimp or Crab with Butter and Garlic

Truly fresh Gulf of Mexico shrimp or blue crab, simply sautéed with garlic and butter, is as sweet and succulent as anything from the Northeast. As a filling for enchiladas or tacos, these shrimp are amazing. We use the succulent crab exclusively for Laguna Madre Enchiladas (page 66).

Makes about 2 cups

1 pound medium shrimp, peeled and deveined; or lump crabmeat, picked over to remove any pieces of shell
1 tablespoon unsalted butter
2 garlic cloves, minced
⅛ teaspoon salt

Use for
Enchiladas Tampico (page 75),
Enchiladas Laguna Madre (page 66),
Tacos (page 101)

Cut each shrimp into 3 pieces. Set aside.

In a medium skillet over medium heat, melt the butter. Add the shrimp (or crabmeat) and garlic and cook, stirring constantly, for 3 minutes, or until the shrimp are barely pink or the crabmeat is heated through. Season with salt.

The Enchilada Queen's Texas Two-Step Secret to Great Enchiladas

The Texas Two-Step is the real secret of my signature enchiladas. First I flavor the tortillas, then I soften them for filling and rolling. Flavoring or spicing the tortillas involves dipping them in a thin chile sauce. The chile sauce uses dried red chiles to give rich, deep flavor and a beautiful tint to tortillas used for enchiladas. Then I soften the tortillas in hot oil before filling and rolling.

Most restaurants don't do this two-step because it is too time-consuming, takes up precious refrigerator space, and drives up overall costs. Most restaurants just dip tortillas in hot oil or heat them on a griddle to make them pliable. Others dip them in whatever sauce is to be used with the dish, perhaps tomatillo sauce or chili gravy.

To achieve optimal flavor, however, you must do each step of this culinary dance to get it right. Two-Step enchiladas are more practical for home preparation because you aren't making hundreds of them as we do at the restaurants, where, after dipping tortillas for enchiladas in chile sauce, we stack the tortillas, cover tightly, and refrigerate overnight. At home, it's okay to shortcut flavoring the tortillas: Dip, stack, and cover them while you're making the sauce and filling. Then soften in hot oil. Fill, roll, sauce, and bake. But, please don't skip the flavoring step. Not if you want enchiladas anywhere near as good as mine.

Great enchiladas are worth it. Enchiladas aren't fast food, but with some planning you can get them done. Making them at home the old-fashioned, authentic way is much like ballroom dancing. Learn each step and follow my lead.

Enchilada Queen Secret Chile Sauce for Flavoring Tortillas

Makes about 1¾ cups, enough to flavor up to 2 dozen tortillas

7 guajillo chiles, stems and seeds removed

2 *chiles de árbol*, stems removed (no need to remove seeds)

Rinse the chiles with cool water.

In a medium saucepan over high heat, combine the chiles and 1¾ cups water. Bring to a boil, then reduce the heat and simmer for 15 minutes. Set aside off the heat for 10 minutes.

In a blender jar or work bowl of a food processor, process the cooked chiles and their liquid until smooth, about 1 minute.

Pour the pureed chile mixture through a fine strainer into a small bowl, pressing with the back of a spoon to extract as much liquid as possible; discard the solids.

Cover the sauce and put in the refrigerator to chill, then use to flavor tortillas (see page 54).

To store and reuse the chile sauce, strain out any pieces of tortilla before pouring into a clean, covered container.

The flavoring sauce may be refrigerated for up to 1 week or frozen for up to 6 months. Thaw completely and stir before using.

Enchilada Queen Texas Two-Step

Up to 24 corn tortillas
Chile Sauce for Flavoring
   Tortillas (see page 53)
1 cup vegetable oil

To Flavor and Soften Corn Tortillas

Dip each tortilla in the chile sauce. Drain off excess liquid. Stack the spiced tortillas on a plate. Cover with plastic wrap or foil. Refrigerate overnight or for as little time as it takes to make the desired enchilada sauce in chapter 3 and filling in chapter 4.

When the sauce and filling are ready and the tortillas are flavored, soften the tortillas for stuffing and rolling: In a medium skillet over medium heat, warm the oil until it shimmers or about 375°F.

Using a nonstick spatula, slide one flavored tortilla at a time into the hot oil, cook for 2 or 3 seconds, then turn it over. When the tortilla is pliable (after another 1 or 2 seconds), remove from the oil immediately so the tortilla doesn't crisp. Tortillas should remain pliable for rolling. The total time in the oil should be no more than 5 seconds.

Stack the softened tortillas on a plate and continue dipping in hot oil until all the flavored tortillas are

softened. Cover the softened flavored tortillas with plastic or foil to keep soft.

Allow the tortillas to cool for 10 minutes or until cool enough to handle. Covered tightly with plastic wrap to prevent drying out, tortillas may sit for as long as an hour. Fill, roll, and bake according to the enchilada recipe.

To Fill and Bake Enchiladas

Once your sauce (see chapter 3) and filling (see chapter 4) are made and the tortillas are spiced and softened, you are ready to assemble enchiladas. Select a baking dish large enough to hold the enchiladas in a single layer with some space in between. This makes it easier to remove baked enchiladas for serving. Usually a 9 × 11-inch baking dish works well. To make clean-up easier, lightly coat the enchilada baking dish with cooking spray.

Set up your assembly line: 1. spiced and softened tortillas 2. warmed filling 3. baking dish 4. warmed sauce and 5. garnishes. *(continued)*

Enchilada Queen Texas Two-Step *(continued)*

Figure 2 (or 3) enchiladas per serving.

Preheat the oven. Heat the desired sauce and filling until warm but do not boil; keep warm.

When all the tortillas have been spiced and softened, place about ⅓ cup (or 2 ounces) shredded cheese or 2 rounded tablespoons of filling in the center of each tortilla. Roll the tortilla around the filling and place in a large baking dish, seam side down. Repeat until all the tortillas are filled. Leave a small space between enchiladas, about ⅛ inch, to make removal from the pan easier.

Pour about ¼ cup sauce over each enchilada and, if recipe calls for it, sprinkle cheese over top of enchiladas. Enchiladas may sit for up to 30 minutes, tightly covered, before baking. Do not refrigerate.

4. Bake according to the recipe. Enchiladas taste best if baked right after filling and saucing.

5. Garnish as the recipe directs. Serve immediately.

About my enchilada names

I named the enchilada combinations on my menu after key towns in borderland Texas and Mexico. These towns are featured on the map (see endpapers). The map is also a key feature in my restaurants, where, as a mural, it takes up most of a wall. Mapping the enchiladas gives you an idea of how blended South Texas is with neighboring Mexico. My Tex-Mex enchiladas are named for Texas cities. Traditional Mexican enchiladas are named after cities in that country.

Tex-Mex Enchiladas

DONNA

Beef with Chili Gravy

Donna is a small town in South Texas with history similar to many in the area. In Hidalgo County (formerly part of the Mexican state of Tamaulipas), the area that is now the city was part of an 1834 Mexico land grant to settlers. The city was founded in 1907 when the location became a train stop with depot. It was named Donna after postmistress Donna Fletcher, who also owned and ran Alameda (Grove) Ranch. These enchiladas are a salute to the ranchers who made beef a staple of Tex-Mex.

Donna is where my mother was born and where my grandparents are laid to rest. It is a special place to me. And this is a special enchilada.   *Makes 12 enchiladas*

3 cups Rio Grande Ground Beef (page 44), warm

12 flavored and softened corn tortillas (page 54)

5 cups Classic Tex-Mex Chili Gravy (page 27), warm

1 cup shredded cheddar cheese

1 cup diced onion (optional), plus more for garnish if desired

Preheat the oven to 425°F. Spray a 9 × 11-inch baking dish with cooking spray.

Place about ¼ cup of the beef in the center of a tortilla. Roll and place seam side down in the baking dish. Repeat until all the tortillas are filled, arranging them in the baking dish with ⅛ inch in between.

Pour ¼ cup sauce over each enchilada, and sprinkle evenly with the cheese and chopped onions, if desired.

Bake for 7 to 10 minutes, until the cheese is melted and the sauce is bubbly.

Garnish with a little more cheese and additional onion, if desired. Serve immediately.

Cheese Enchiladas with Chili Gravy

The small town of Refugio is halfway between Brownsville, the southern tip of Texas, and Houston, farther up the Gulf Coast, where I live. It's a typical small South Texas town, very Tex-Mex. That's why I call my customers' favorite enchilada the Refugio.

About the name: In Texas, we say "re-FURY-oh." Where'd that "r" sound come from? Legend has it that way back when the train stopped in Refugio, the Irish conductor couldn't pronounce "re-FU-heoh," with an "h" sound the *español* way, so he called it "re-FURY-oh" and it's been pronounced that way ever since.

For Tex-Mex-style cheese enchiladas, yellow cheese, such as cheddar, is the traditional choice. Combined with my amazing Chili Gravy, this is the quintessential Tex-Mex enchilada.

Makes 12 enchiladas

4 cups shredded cheddar cheese, plus 1 ¼ cups for garnish

12 flavored and softened corn tortillas (page 54)

5 cups Classic Tex-Mex Chili Gravy (page 27), warm

1 cup diced onion (optional)

Preheat the oven to 425°F. Spray a 9 × 11-inch baking dish with cooking spray.

Place about ⅓ cup of the cheese in the center of a tortilla. Roll and place seam side down in the baking dish. Repeat until all the tortillas are filled, arranging them in baking dish with ⅛ inch in between.

Pour ¼ cup sauce over each enchilada, and sprinkle evenly with grated cheese and onion, if desired.

Bake for 7 to 10 minutes, until the cheese is melted and the sauce is bubbly.

Garnish with a little more cheese. Serve immediately.

Chicken with Chili Gravy

One of the largest in the region, McAllen is another Lower Rio Grande Valley city. It is named after what eventually became McAllen Ranch, still a working cattle ranch. The ranch's title has been held by the same family since 1790 and was part of Nuevo Santander, or Wild Horse Desert. Salome Young, a female descendant of the original land grant holder, José Manuel Gómez, married John McAllen in 1861. In 1980, the McAllen Ranch was recognized by the State of Texas' Family Land Heritage program, which honors families that have owned and continuously operated a farm or ranch for a hundred years or more.

Even when filled with chicken, enchiladas in this part of the state are usually sauced with Chili Gravy.

Makes 12 enchiladas

3 cups *Pollo Guisado* (page 45) or Stewed Chicken Breast (page 46), warm

12 flavored and softened corn tortillas (page 54)

5 cups Classic Tex-Mex Chili Gravy (page 27), warm

1 cup shredded Monterey Jack cheese, plus more for garnish if desired

Preheat the oven to 425°F. Spray a 9 × 11-inch baking dish with cooking spray.

Place about ¼ cup of the chicken in the center of a tortilla. Roll and place seam side down in the baking dish. Repeat until all the tortillas are filled, arranging them in the baking dish with ⅛ inch in between.

Pour ¼ cup sauce over each enchilada, and sprinkle evenly with the cheese.

Bake for 7 to 10 minutes, until the cheese is melted and the sauce is bubbly.

Garnish with a little more cheese, if desired. Serve immediately.

Beef or Chicken Fajita with Chili Gravy

The name of this enchilada pays tribute to the famous King Ranch, perhaps the best-known ranch in Texas. Named after legendary rancher Richard King, even today the spread, though not as massive as it once was, is larger than the state of Rhode Island. King began amassing land in South Texas in 1853. On a cattle-buying trip to Mexico, King recruited approximately a hundred men, women, and children to return with him to work on the ranch. Since those days, King Ranch workers and associates have been known as *los Kineños*, or King's men.

That makes the name particularly appropriate for this enchilada filled with fajitas, made with a cooking technique that originated on frontera cattle ranches. **Makes 12 enchiladas**

3 cups Beef or Chicken Fajita (page 108), warm

12 flavored and softened corn tortillas (page 54)

5 cups Classic Tex-Mex Chili Gravy (page 27), warm

1 cup shredded cheddar cheese, plus more for garnish if desired

Preheat the oven to 425°F. Spray a 9 × 11-inch baking dish with cooking spray.

Place about ¼ cup of the beef or chicken in the center of a tortilla. Roll and place seam side down in the baking dish. Repeat until all the tortillas are filled, arranging them in the baking dish with ⅛ inch in between.

Pour ¼ cup sauce over each enchilada, and sprinkle evenly with the cheese.

Bake for 7 to 10 minutes, until the cheese is melted and the sauce is bubbly.

Garnish with a little more cheese, if desired. Serve immediately.

Rio Grande Ground Beef or Cheese and Onions with Chili Gravy or *Salsa Roja*

El Paso marks the far western boundary of our state, where New Mexico and the Mexican state of Chihuahua intersect. An old Texas city with a storied history, El Paso has a sibling city on the other side of the Rio Grande, Ciudad Juarez. If it weren't for a river that became a border, there might not be two cities. The same goes for Matamoros and Brownsville; Laredo and Nuevo Laredo.

Located in the Chihuahuan desert, this portion of the Rio Grande is often compared to the Nile. In many ways, El Paso is more Mexican and New Mexican than Texan. In that sense it is a truly international city.

This stacked style of enchilada is classic El Paso, reflecting the New Mexico enchilada tradition. I added it to my menu by popular demand from El Paso natives who had moved to Houston. I spent about two months preparing and taste paneling the prototype with two customers who were El Paso natives. When an elderly lady who had moved to Houston with her daughter finally "blessed" my version, I added it to the menu.

El Paso enchiladas are classically offered with an option of Chili Gravy or *Salsa Roja* and filled with either ground beef or cheddar cheese blended with chopped onions. Mix and match however you like.

Often those who order this enchilada want a fried egg on top. Native El Pasoans also like a side garnish of shredded lettuce and tomatoes.

These should be assembled on individual ovenproof plates for heating and serving. Or use two 9 × 13-inch baking dishes or lasagna pans and assemble three stacked enchiladas in each. Use a large spatula to transfer to a serving plate.

Makes 6 enchiladas

Rio Grande Ground Beef or Cheese and Onions with Chili Gravy or *Salsa Roja* (continued)

18 spiced and softened corn tortillas (page 54)

2 cups Rio Grande Ground Beef (page 44), warm; or 4 cups shredded cheddar cheese blended with 1½ cups diced onions

4 cups Classic Tex-Mex Chili Gravy (page 27) or *Salsa Roja* (page 29), warm

1 cup shredded cheddar cheese

6 fried eggs (optional)

4 cups shredded iceberg lettuce (optional)

1 cup finely chopped tomatoes (optional)

Preheat the oven to 425°F.

On an ovenproof plate, or baking dish, place one tortilla in the center. Add about ¼ cup ground beef or ½ cup cheese and onion blend; spread filling evenly to edge of tortilla.

Top with a second tortilla and repeat step with desired filling.

Place a third tortilla on top of the filling. Pour ½ cup of the sauce over the top of the tortilla. Sprinkle with 2 to 3 tablespoons of the cheese.

Place the plate or plates in the oven and bake for 7 to 10 minutes, until the sauce bubbles.

If desired, top each stacked enchilada with a fried egg right after it comes out of the oven and add a side of shredded lettuce and chopped tomatoes on the plate. Serve immediately.

Spinach with *Salsa Verde*

The Lower Rio Grande Valley is the truck garden of Texas. South of San Antonio, Crystal City proudly calls itself the Spinach Capital. Hence my name for spinach enchiladas. Filled with sautéed spinach, these enchiladas are favorites for anyone going meatless for the meal, the day, or forever.

Makes 12 enchiladas

3 cups shredded Monterey Jack cheese

Spinach (page 50), warm

12 spiced and softened corn tortillas (page 54)

4 cups *Salsa Verde* (page 38), warm

Preheat oven to 425°F. Spray a 9 × 11-inch baking dish with cooking spray.

Place about 1 tablespoon of the cheese and 2 tablespoons of the spinach filling in the center of a tortilla. Roll and place seam side down in the baking dish. Repeat until all the tortillas are filled, arranging them in the baking dish with ⅛ inch in between.

Pour ¼ cup sauce over each enchilada and sprinkle evenly with the remaining cheese.

Bake for 7 to 10 minutes, until the cheese is melted and the sauce is bubbly. Serve immediately.

Crab with *Salsa de Jaiba*

Laguna Madre is a salty lagoon that runs along the coast of South Texas, part of the Gulf of Mexico. It stretches south from Corpus Christi to Brownsville including Padre Island National Seashore. It is a breeding ground for Gulf Coast fish species such as sea trout and redfish, as well as shrimp and crabs. The Laguna Madre system is the only hypersaline coastal lagoon in North America and one of only five in the world. It is a Texas treasure and a seafood lover's happy place, so I named my very special crab enchiladas after it. The addition of cheese to the crab enchilada filling binds the crabmeat so the filling holds together.   *Makes 12 enchiladas*

16 ounces Crab with Butter and Garlic (page 51), warm

12 spiced and softened corn tortillas (page 54)

1 cup shredded Monterey Jack cheese

3 cups *Salsa de Jaiba* (page 41), warm

12 slices avocado

Preheat the oven to 425°F. Spray a 9 × 11-inch baking dish with cooking spray.

Place 2 tablespoons of the crab in the center of a tortilla. Add 1 tablespoon of the cheese. Roll and place seam side down in the baking dish. Repeat until all the tortillas are filled, arranging them in the baking dish with ⅛ inch in between.

Pour ¼ cup sauce over each enchilada.

Bake for 7 to 10 minutes, until the sauce is bubbly.

Garnish each enchilada with a slice of avocado. Serve immediately.

Calabacitas and Maiz with Salsa de Crema

Sarita is a tiny town in the middle of the vast acreage of the original King Ranch. I named this enchilada after the village in honor of my grandmother, also named Sarita. (Darn it, our family is not related to the fabulously wealthy King Ranch heir for whom the town was named.) Mamá Grande Sarita was a humble, hardworking woman whose cooking inspired much of this book.

The filling in this enchilada reminds me of a dish both my mother and grandmother fixed. As a kid, I loved when they made *calabacitas* with chicken or pork for dinner. *Calabacitas* are Mexican squash, similar to zucchini, but a lighter shade of green, a little shorter and wider. We had this delicious skillet meal on a weekly basis along with beans and flour or corn tortillas. I was in heaven every time they prepared it.

I adapted my favorite dinner dish to be a meatless enchilada filling in answer to many customer requests. To my great delight, one of my "meatless" customers described the Sarita enchilada as "a symphony of flavors."

Makes 6 servings

---

2 cups *Calabacitas* and *Maiz* (page 49), warm

12 spiced and softened corn tortillas (page 54)

3 cups *Salsa de Crema* (page 40), warm

¾ cup very finely diced tomato, rinsed and drained well to remove seeds

Preheat the oven to 425°F. Spray a 9 × 11-inch baking dish with cooking spray.

Place about 3 tablespoons of the filling in the center of a tortilla. Roll and place seam side down in the baking dish. Repeat until all the tortillas are filled, arranging them in the baking dish with ⅛ inch in between.

Pour ¼ cup sauce over each enchilada.

Bake for 7 to 10 minutes, until the sauce is bubbly.

Garnish each enchilada with about 1 tablespoon tomato just before serving. Serve immediately.

Mex-Mex Enchiladas

 Chicken with *Salsa Suiza*

San Miguel is one of my favorite cities in Mexico, and this "white enchilada" is also a Mexican favorite. Filled with chicken and sauced with a creamy tomatillo sauce, this style of enchilada is popular all over Mexico. Located in the eastern part of the country in the state of Guanajuato, San Miguel de Allende is famed for its Spanish colonial architecture and its artist community. Hence I named this beautiful enchilada after a beautiful city. **Makes 12 enchiladas**

2 cups Stewed Chicken Breast (page 46), warm

12 spiced and softened corn tortillas (page 54)

3 cups *Salsa Suiza* (page 37), warm

3 cups shredded Monterey Jack cheese

1 cup finely shredded iceberg lettuce

1 cup shredded *queso fresco*

1 red onion, thinly sliced into rounds

Preheat the oven to 425°F. Spray a 9 × 11-inch baking dish with cooking spray.

Place 2 tablespoons of the chicken in the center of a tortilla. Roll and place seam side down in the baking dish. Repeat until all the tortillas are filled, arranging them in the baking dish with ⅛ inch in between.

Pour ¼ cup sauce over each enchilada and sprinkle evenly with the Monterey Jack.

Bake for 7 to 10 minutes, until the cheese is melted and the sauce is bubbly.

Garnish the enchiladas with the lettuce, *queso fresco*, and onions. Serve immediately.

Chicken with *Salsa Verde*

In Mexico, if you say "enchilada," spicy stewed chicken filling with *Salsa Verde* is what many people think of first. This is the classic Mexican enchilada; hence I named it after the capital of the country. Mexico City or simply *Ciudad*, as it's known south of the border, is in the center of Mexico and is the heart of the country.

While most enchiladas can be made up to 30 minutes before baking, enchiladas with *Salsa Verde* should be rolled, sauced, and baked immediately or the acid in the tomatillos will break down the tortillas.

Makes 12 enchiladas

2 cups *Pollo Guisado* (page 45), warm

12 spiced and softened corn tortillas (page 54)

3 cups *Salsa Verde* (page 38), warm

1¼ cups shredded Chihuahua or Monterey Jack cheese

1 pint sour cream

Preheat the oven to 425°F. Spray a 9 × 11-inch baking dish with cooking spray.

Place 2 tablespoons of the chicken in the center of a tortilla. Roll and place seam side down in the baking dish. Repeat until all the tortillas are filled, arranging them in the baking dish with ⅛ inch in between.

Pour ¼ cup sauce over each enchilada and sprinkle evenly with the cheese.

Bake for 7 to 10 minutes, until the cheese is melted and the sauce is bubbly.

Top each enchilada with about 2 tablespoons sour cream. Serve immediately.

White Cheese with *Salsa Guajillo*

Morelia, deep in the center of the country, is a typical small Mexican town and this is a very classic, very rustic enchilada sauced with a deep, red sauce made from guajillo chiles. The combination is a favorite all over Mexico, New Mexico, and the Texas border region. My mother used to call these "Mexican enchiladas."

This recipe uses traditional white Mexican cheese, *queso fresco*, which literally means "fresh cheese." Mild and milky in flavor, it is a great complement to the smoky dried chile sauce. The characteristic salty-sour kick, similar to very mild goat cheese or feta, is a favorite in Mexico and along the Rio Grande. Because it is low in fat, *queso fresco* does not melt.   **Makes 12 enchiladas**

2 cups shredded *queso fresco*

1 white onion, diced

12 spiced and softened corn tortillas (page 54)

3 cups *Salsa Roja* (page 29), warm

2 cups thinly shredded Romaine lettuce

6 to 7 radishes, thinly sliced

½ small red onion, thinly sliced

Preheat the oven to 425°F. Spray a 9 × 11-inch baking dish with cooking spray.

In a small bowl, combine 1½ cups of the cheese and the white onion. Place about 2 tablespoons of the mixture in the center of a tortilla. Roll and place seam side down in the baking dish. Repeat until all the tortillas are filled, arranging them in the baking dish with ⅛ inch in between.

Pour ¼ cup sauce over each enchilada.

Bake for 7 to 10 minutes, until bubbly. (*Queso fresco* will not melt because it is very low in fat.)

Garnish with the remaining ½ cup cheese, the lettuce, radishes, and red onion. Serve immediately.

Shrimp with *Salsa Veracruzana*

Tampico is a famous Mexican coastal town on the Gulf side. It is famous for shrimp and fish dishes. These shrimp enchiladas are beautiful with a Mediterranean-style tomato sauce. With very mild spice, the sauce is a culinary *amigo* to fish because *Salsa Veracruzana* complements instead of covering the taste of truly fresh seafood.   **Makes 8 enchiladas**

2 cups Shrimp with Butter and Garlic (page 51), warm

8 spiced and softened corn tortillas (page 54)

1 cup shredded Chihuahua or Monterey Jack cheese

2 cups *Salsa Veracruzana* (page 36), warm

Preheat the oven to 425°F. Spray a 9 × 11-inch baking dish with cooking spray.

Place 6 to 8 pieces of shrimp in the center of a tortilla and add 1 tablespoon of the cheese. Roll and place seam side down in the baking dish. Repeat until all the tortillas are filled, arranging them in the baking dish with ⅛ inch in between.

Pour ¼ cup sauce over each enchilada.

Bake for 7 to 10 minutes, until the sauce is bubbly. Serve immediately.

Chicken, Beef, or Cheese with *Salsa Española*

The third largest city in Mexico is about two hundred miles west of Brownsville, Texas. Monterrey, Mexico (not spelled like Monterey, California), is a major business hub. I named this enchilada "Monterrey" because the city is relatively close to the border with Texas and so many flavors popular in the border region are also enjoyed in Monterrey. This enchilada's relatively mild sauce is very common and beloved in Mexico and the Texas border area. Typically filled with *Pollo Guisado*, Rio Grande Ground Beef or Monterey Jack cheese may also be used as fillings.

Makes 12 enchiladas

3 cups *Pollo Guisado* (page 45) or Rio Grande Beef (page 44), warm; or 3 cups shredded Monterey Jack or Chihuahua cheese

12 spiced and softened corn tortillas (page 54)

3 cups *Salsa Española* (page 35), warm

1¼ cups shredded Monterey Jack or Chihuahua cheese

Preheat the oven to 425°F. Spray a 9 × 11-inch baking dish with cooking spray.

Place ¼ cup of the chicken, beef, or cheese in the center of a tortilla. Roll and place seam side down in the baking dish. Repeat until all the tortillas are filled, arranging them in the baking dish with ⅛ inch in between.

Pour ¼ cup sauce over each enchilada and sprinkle evenly with cheese.

Bake for 7 to 10 minutes, until the cheese is melted and the sauce is bubbly. Serve immediately.

White Cheese, *Pollo Guisado*, or Rio Grande Ground Beef with *Salsa Ranchera*

The northern Mexico state of Chihuahua bumps up against Texas and New Mexico. The state capital is Ciudad Chihuahua. The kinship among this part of Mexico, Texas, and New Mexico is close, especially in terms of cuisine. These enchiladas may be made with chicken or beef, even white cheese. The sauce is tomato-based and spicy with jalapeños. **Makes 12 enchiladas**

3 cups shredded Monterey Jack cheese, or warm *Pollo Guisado* (page 45) or Rio Grande Ground Beef (page 44)

12 spiced and softened corn tortillas (page 54)

3 cups *Salsa Ranchera* (page 31), warm

1¼ cups shredded Monterey Jack cheese

Preheat the oven to 425°F. Spray a 9 × 11-inch baking dish with cooking spray.

Place 3 tablespoons of the cheese, chicken, or ground beef in the center of a tortilla. Roll and place seam side down in the baking dish. Repeat until all the tortillas are filled, arranging them in the baking dish with ⅛ inch in between.

Pour ¼ cup sauce over each enchilada and sprinkle evenly with cheese.

Bake for 7 to 10 minutes, until the cheese is melted and the sauce is bubbly. Serve immediately.

Stewed Chicken Breast with *Mole Poblano*

Puebla is the home of *mole poblano* and the events that led to the celebration of Mexican independence from France, today known as Cinco de Mayo. *Mole* sauce is the signature of the city and region's cooking. There are hundreds of variations on this rich, spicy sauce usually made with chocolate, cinnamon, and ground nuts as well as various dried peppers. Although *mole* is traditionally served over braised chicken pieces, I developed a chicken enchilada for my *mole* sauce.

Makes 12 enchiladas

3 cups Stewed Chicken Breast (page 46), warm

12 spiced and softened corn tortillas (page 54)

3 cups *Mole Poblano* (page 32), warm

1¼ cups shredded Monterey Jack or Chihuahua cheese

Preheat the oven to 425°F. Spray a 9 × 11-inch baking dish with cooking spray.

Place 3 tablespoons of the chicken in the center of a tortilla. Roll and place seam side down in the baking dish. Repeat until all the tortillas are filled, arranging them in the baking dish with ⅛ inch in between.

Pour ¼ cup sauce over each enchilada and sprinkle evenly with cheese.

Bake for 7 to 10 minutes, until the cheese is melted and the sauce is bubbly. Serve immediately.

Carnitas with *Salsa de Crema Verde*

Hidalgo, for which I named this enchilada, is a state in Mexico in the eastern part of the country and it is known for dishes with both red and green sauces. *Carnitas* (pork) enchiladas combine well with tangy and slightly spicy and creamy *Salsa de Crema Verde*. A touch of sour cream and a little avocado enrich and smooth the tomatillo salsa, which pairs so beautifully with crispy morsels of pork.

Makes 12 enchiladas

2 cups *Carnitas* (page 47), warm

12 spiced and softened corn tortillas (page 54)

3 cups *Salsa Hidalgo Verde* (page 39), warm

1¼ cups shredded Monterey Jack or Chihuahua cheese

Preheat the oven to 425°F. Spray a 9 × 11-inch baking dish with cooking spray.

Place 3 tablespoons of the *Carnitas* in the center of a tortilla. Roll and place seam side down in the baking dish. Repeat until all the tortillas are filled, arranging them in the baking dish with ⅛ inch in between.

Pour ¼ cup sauce over each enchilada and sprinkle evenly with cheese.

Bake for 7 to 10 minutes, until the cheese is melted and the sauce is bubbly. Serve immediately.

Carnitas (Slow-Fried Pork) with Salsa Hidalgo Roja

This enchilada is the regional sibling of the *de Crema Verde*. I created this very spicy sauce to go with *carnitas*. *Roja* is the spiciest of all my enchilada sauces. My version of the sauce was developed using *chiles pequin*. They are popular and grow wild all over South Texas and northern Mexico. More widely available *chiles de árbol* may also be used. This is a very popular Mexican-style enchilada.

Makes 12 enchiladas

2 cups *Carnitas* (page 47), warm

12 spiced and softened corn tortillas (page 54)

2 cups shredded Monterey Jack cheese

3 cups *Salsa Hidalgo Roja* (page 30), warm

Preheat the oven to 425°F. Spray a 9 × 11-inch baking dish with cooking spray.

Place 3 tablespoons of the *Carnitas* and 1 tablespoon of the cheese in the center of a tortilla. Roll and place seam side down in the baking dish. Repeat until all the tortillas are filled (reserve the remaining cheese), arranging them in the baking dish with ⅛ inch in between.

Pour ¼ cup sauce over each enchilada and sprinkle evenly with the reserved cheese.

Bake for 7 to 10 minutes, until the cheese is melted and the sauce is bubbly. Serve immediately.

Chicken with *Salsa Casera*

Known as the second city of Mexico, Guadalajara is the home of mariachis and tequila. I named this chicken enchilada in honor of one of my favorite employees, Luis Montes, who comes from Guadalajara. He described this mild, marinara-style sauce as tasting "so much like home."

Makes 12 enchiladas

2 cups *Pollo Guisado* (page 45), warm

12 spiced and softened corn tortillas (page 54)

3 cups *Salsa Casera* (page 34), warm

2 cups finely shredded iceberg lettuce

2 medium tomatoes, thickly sliced

1 cup shredded *queso fresco*

Preheat the oven to 425°F. Spray a 9 × 11-inch baking dish with cooking spray.

Place 3 tablespoons of the chicken in the center of a tortilla. Roll and place seam side down in the baking dish. Repeat until all the tortillas are filled, arranging them in the baking dish with ⅛ inch in between.

Pour ¼ cup sauce over each enchilada.

Bake for 7 to 10 minutes, until bubbly.

Just before serving, garnish each enchilada with a sprinkle of lettuce, a piece of tomato, and 1 tablespoon cheese. Serve immediately.

CHAPTER 5

SALSAS, APPETIZERS, AND SNACKS

"Chips and salsa" is a signature of Tex-Mex. In South Texas and the rest of the state, every "Mexican restaurant"—as they are usually called—offers complimentary chips with salsa to every customer. This is a totally Tex-Mex, not Mexican, tradition. In a typical restaurant in Mexico, a basket of chips and a bowl of salsa don't automatically appear on the table even before you're handed a menu. However, in a "Mexican restaurant" in Texas, a meal of "Mexican food" *must* begin with the gut-busting habit of a basket of chips with salsa in anticipation of a plate of enchiladas. I've actually had people complain to me that they can't get "real Mexican food" in Mexico because restaurants south of the border don't automatically serve chips and salsa.

Notice that I've referred to "Mexican food" and "Mexican restaurants" in Texas. Not Tex-Mex. That's because Texans don't go out for "Tex-Mex." Texans go out to a "Mexican restaurant" for "Mexican food," although we know perfectly well that what we want is Tex-Mex, not authentic "Mexican food" as it would be found in Mexico. When Texans want that, they seek a place serving "interior Mexican food" or "Mex-Mex."

One more irony about the food I serve: Many customers swear they love my food "because it isn't Tex-Mex." I've got news for

them. What they may think of as Tex-Mex is just lower quality, gloppy, brown plates crowned by mounds of cheese. That to me isn't true Tex-Mex. What I serve, using fresh ingredients and fresh, housemade sauces, reflects the quality and style of Texas-Mexican cooking I grew up eating, at home and in restaurants.

Back to the beginning of a meal at Sylvia's: When it comes to Tex-Mex, chips and salsa are mandatory. Many customers claim that the quality of chips and salsa sets the standard for any Tex-Mex eatery. That's a challenge I take seriously. My chips are crisp and freshly fried daily, served warm, alongside gently warmed *Salsa de Mesa* (Table Salsa) (page 85).

In terms of spice, my salsas range from mild to "hair on fire." My basic *Salsa de Mesa* falls somewhere in between. It's got some piquancy but it doesn't set the palate ablaze. There are several other salsas in this chapter that go all the way up to by-special-order-only "Hair on Fire" Habanero Salsa (page 88).

Of course, Tex-Mex starters go well beyond chips and salsa. *Chile con queso* (cheese dip) and guacamole are other favorites used for chip dipping. And there are dishes to share at the beginning of a meal, usually beginning with a tortilla, such as *flautas* or nachos.

Salsa de Mesa

TABLE SALSA

I serve warm *Salsa de Mesa* with chips in my restaurants. This salsa may be served at room temperature if desired, but the fresh and vibrant flavors really come through best when served warm. That's why I heat it gently before serving. This recipe may be modified in various ways. One simple way to add another flavor dimension is to roast the tomatoes and jalapeño first. Then just follow the recipe.

Makes about 4 cups

10 vine-ripened Roma tomatoes (roasted, if desired; see below), cut in half

4 *chiles pequin* or *chiles de árbol*, stems removed (no need to remove seeds)

½ jalapeño, cut in half lengthwise (roasted, if desired; see below)

4 garlic cloves, smashed

1 cup chopped white onion

½ cup chopped fresh cilantro leaves

1½ teaspoons salt

In a medium saucepan over high heat, combine the tomatoes, dried chiles, jalapeño, garlic, onion, and 1¼ cups water. Bring to a boil, then reduce the heat to very low and simmer for about 20 minutes, or until all the ingredients are soft. Set aside off the heat to cool for 10 minutes.

In a blender jar or work bowl of a food processor, combine the cooked mixture, cilantro, and salt. Process for about 1 minute, until smooth.

Serve warm or at room temperature.

The salsa may be refrigerated for up to 1 week or frozen for up to 3 months.

To roast the tomatoes and jalapeño

Place the vegetables on a broiler pan or in a heavy skillet. Place under the broiler at 500°F or over high heat. Cook until the skin is puffed and browned or blackened, turning as needed, for about 5 minutes. Do not peel.

Frontera Pico de Gallo Salsa
FRESH BORDER SALSA

Unlike my *Salsa de Mesa*, this salsa is uncooked, a style known as *pico de gallo*, which literally translates to "rooster's beak." The origins of the name aren't well documented. I've always considered it a Spanish play on words reflecting the small size of the chopped ingredients, something a chicken could peck at. *Pico* means "beak" and *picar* means "to chop."

No matter how *pico* got its unusual name, *pico de gallo* is a classic addition to fajitas. Makes sense, since fajitas originated on ranches where it was more likely that ranch hands could more easily chop up fresh vegetables to create a *salsa* rather than haul around jars of cooked salsa.

When preparing this recipe, pay attention to the size of the chopped vegetables. They should be cut small and uniform in size. The jalapeño should be very finely minced so as not to burn the mouth. If less heat is desired, remove about half of the jalapeño seeds before chopping. You can always add them back if the salsa is not sufficiently spicy. The heat of this recipe is moderate to most tastes. Of course, remember to wear plastic food handlers' gloves when working with fresh chiles. It is easier to remove and throw away the gloves than it is to wash the volatile oils from your hands and fingers.

If the *pico de gallo* is "wet" or very juicy after blending all the ingredients, place the *pico* in a strainer over the sink or a bowl and drain for a few minutes.   **Makes about 5 cups**

2 large tomatoes, cut into ¼-inch pieces to make about 2½ cups

1 large yellow onion, peeled and cut into ¼-inch pieces to make about 2 cups

1 (4-inch-long) jalapeño, cut into very small pieces (seeded if very mild *pico de gallo* is desired)

½ cup (lightly packed) fresh cilantro leaves, chopped to ¼ inch

¾ teaspoon salt

2 teaspoons fresh lime juice (optional)

Place the tomatoes in a strainer, rinse, and drain.

In a medium bowl, combine the drained tomatoes, onion, jalapeño, and cilantro. Add salt and lime juice, if desired. Gently stir the ingredients to blend well.

Cover with plastic wrap and, if time allows, store in the refrigerator for about 30 minutes before serving. Otherwise, serve immediately.

The salsa may be refrigerated for up to 1 week. Do not freeze.

Enchilada Queen *Salsa de Casa*

This is a salsa variation that includes tomatillos. I serve this at home for family. It is very good with chips or any Tex-Mex dish. The tomatoes, husked tomatillos, and jalapeño may also be roasted if that's a flavor variation you want to try.

Makes about 2 cups

2 pounds vine-ripened
    tomatoes, cut into 4 pieces
    (roasted, if desired; see
    below)

3 tomatillos, rinsed after
    peeling papery outer skin
    (roasted, if desired; see
    below)

4 *chiles de árbol*, stems removed

½ or 1 whole jalapeño,
    depending on desired heat
    (roasted, if desired; see
    below)

½ cup chopped white onion

3 garlic cloves, chopped

2 to 4 tablespoons chopped
    fresh cilantro leaves

1½ teaspoons salt

In a medium saucepan over high heat, combine the tomatoes, tomatillos, dried chiles, jalapeño, and 1¼ cups water. Bring to a boil, then reduce heat and simmer for 20 minutes. Set aside off the heat to cool for 10 minutes.

In a blender jar or work bowl of a food processor, process the cooked mixture, onion, garlic, cilantro, and salt for about 1 minute, until smooth. Adjust salt as needed.

Serve warm or at room temperature.

The salsa may be refrigerated for up to 1 week or frozen for up to 3 months.

To roast the tomatoes, tomatillos, and jalapeño

Place the vegetables on a broiler pan or in a heavy skillet. Place under the broiler at 500°F or over high heat. Cook until the skin is puffed and browned or blackened, turning as needed, for about 5 minutes. Do not peel.

"Hair on Fire" Habanero Salsa

This table salsa is truly hot, hot, hot! Served only by special request in my restaurants, "Hair on Fire" isn't for the faint of palate. The flavors are complex and layered. Yes, it is very spicy, but it isn't only about the heat. And this recipe can be modified in various ways. One simple way to add another flavor dimension is to roast and blacken the tomatoes and garlic before blending into the salsa. You can mute some of the spice by using fewer habaneros or spike it by using the maximum . . . or more if you dare.

This salsa may be served warm, chilled, or at room temperature, but the fresh and vibrant flavors really come through when served warm. Serve with tortilla chips or over your favorite Tex-Mex dish.

Makes about 6 cups

4 tomatoes, quartered (roasted, if desired; see below), about 2 cups
2 *chiles de árbol*, stems removed
½ medium jalapeño, cut in half lengthwise
2 garlic cloves, smashed (roasted, if desired; see below)
¾ cup chopped white onion
1 teaspoon salt
¼ cup chopped fresh cilantro
3 to 4 habanero chiles, stems removed

In a medium saucepan over high heat, combine the tomatoes, dried chiles, jalapeño, ¾ cup water, the garlic, onion, salt, and cilantro. Bring to a boil over high heat, then reduce the heat and simmer for about 20 minutes, until all the ingredients are soft and well blended. Set aside off the heat.

Place the habaneros on a paper towel and microwave on high power for about 30 seconds.

In a blender jar, combine the cooked tomato mixture and microwaved habaneros. Process on high speed for about 1 minute, until the mixture is smooth.

Set aside to cool a bit before serving. For maximum flavor, serve lukewarm.

The salsa may be refrigerated for up to 1 week or frozen for up to 3 months.

To roast the tomatoes and garlic

Place the vegetables on a broiler pan or in a heavy skillet. Place under the broiler at 500°F or over high heat. Cook until the tomato skin is puffed and browned or blackened, turning as needed, for 3 to 5 minutes. Do not peel. Smash the garlic cloves.

# Fresh Guacamole

Avocados have been called *mantequilla de pobres*, butter of the poor. And no wonder, because a ripe avocado spreads like butter. A schmear of avocado adds a lovely smooth taste to a plain tortilla. I make very basic guacamole because the less I do to an avocado, the better I like it. A little salt and some tomato for color make classic guacamole. Guacamole is more about the quality of the avocados than the recipe. Get *really* good avocados.

If you want to squeeze a bit of lime juice into your guacamole, please do. I don't make it that way because I adore the pure flavor of avocados.

Makes 3 cups, about 6 servings

2 cups finely chopped tomato

3 ripe avocados (see Enchilada Queen Avocado Wisdom, page 90), to make about 2½ cups mashed

1 teaspoon salt

Place the tomatoes in a strainer, rinse, and drain.

In a medium bowl, use a potato masher to mash the avocados until nearly smooth. Add the drained tomatoes to the mashed avocado. Mix well.

Add the salt and adjust seasoning to taste.

Enchilada Queen avocado wisdom

I prefer to make guacamole with Mexican-grown avocados, if available, because they taste more buttery. The smaller Mexican avocados are rough-skinned and dark, even black in color. Avocados imported from Mexico are better than Mexican varieties grown in Florida, although they will do. In general, I prefer avocados from Mexico or Florida. However, any good, ripe avocado—grown wherever—is better than no avocado.

1. Select avocados that are firm but not hard. Check for ripeness by gently pressing your thumb into the side of the avocado. The avocado should yield slightly but not feel soft or mushy.

2. The exterior should be nearly black, not bright green.

3. If the avocados are too firm, allow them to ripen at room temperature for 24 hours. The skin should turn from green to nearly black and yield slightly to the touch. If the avocado is still firm, allow to sit at room temperature for another 24 hours.

4. If an avocado is becoming ripe, you can refrigerate it to slow down the ripening process by a day or so.

5. Placing the avocado seed in the guacamole will not prevent browning. While the addition of lime juice is great for flavor, it does not prevent browning either. The best way to keep guacamole from turning brown is to place plastic wrap directly on the surface to block as much air as possible, then refrigerate. If the guacamole turns a little brown on top, stir to mix. It will look and taste terrific. No one will ever imagine there was ever slight browning!

Enchilada Queen Avocado Salsa Dip

This dip, great for parties, retains its bright green color because of the addition of spinach. Of course, tortilla chips are a must with this dip, but it is also a great match for vegetable crudités and pita chips. My favorite veggie for this dip? Jicama sticks. We use this recipe for many of our catering gigs. Adjust the heat by adding more or less jalapeño. Serve chilled.   **Makes 4 cups**

2 cups chicken broth (page 18)

½ large white onion, cut into four pieces; plus ¼ cup diced onion

3 garlic cloves, smashed

2 large avocados, cut in half (See Enchilada Queen Avocado Wisdom, page 90)

2 tablespoons fresh squeezed lime juice

1 ounce cream cheese, coarsely chopped

¼ cup *crema* or crème fraîche

½ cup finely chopped cilantro leaves

¼ cup finely chopped fresh spinach

½ to 1 large jalapeño, seeded (if desired) and chopped

1 teaspoon salt

In a medium saucepan over high heat, combine the broth, onion, and garlic. Bring to a boil, then lower the heat and simmer for about 10 minutes, until the onion is tender. Set aside off the heat to cool to room temperature, about 20 minutes. To make this go faster, place the saucepan in a large bowl or pan of ice water.

In a blender jar, combine the avocados, lime juice, and 1 cup of the cooled broth (leaving the onion and garlic behind). Process at high speed until the avocados are smooth.

Add the remaining broth (discard the onion and garlic), the cream cheese, *crema*, diced onion, cilantro, spinach, jalapeño, and salt. Process at medium speed for about 30 seconds and then on high until smooth.

Chill for at least 1 hour before serving. May be made early in the day but should be served same day.

Picamole

Picamole is one of my signature recipes. I call it this because it is a hybrid *pico de gallo* and guacamole. The ingredients for *pico de gallo* combine with chunks of avocado to produce Picamole. Any dish that goes well with guacamole and *pico de gallo* is a great fit for Picamole. My customers love it as a dip for chips.

   Precisely cut tomato, onion, and avocado give this dish its somewhat deconstructed appearance with distinct but well-balanced flavors. Picamole is delicious and beautiful.   **Makes 2 cups**

1 cup tomato chopped into
   ⅓-inch cubes
¾ cup yellow onion chopped
   into ⅓-inch cubes
1 (3-inch-long) jalapeño,
   minced (seeded, if desired, to
   lessen the heat), about ⅛ cup
½ cup chopped fresh cilantro
   leaves
2 teaspoons fresh lime juice
½ teaspoon salt
2 ripe avocados (see Enchilada
   Queen Avocado Wisdom,
   page 90), peeled and
   chopped into ½-inch cubes,
   about 2½ cups

Place the tomato in a strainer, rinse, and drain.

In a medium bowl, combine the drained tomato, onion, jalapeño, cilantro, and lime juice. Sprinkle with salt. Using a rubber spatula, combine gently.

Using a rubber spatula, gently fold in the avocados.

Tightly cover the Picamole with plastic wrap directly on the surface to make it airtight.

The Picamole may be refrigerated a couple of hours before serving. Do not freeze.

Enchilada Queen *Chile con Queso* Ⓥ

Lovers of Tex-Mex adore *chile con queso*. What's not to love about melted cheese with a touch of spice? *Queso*, as most Texans call it, is the ultimate dip for tortilla chips. CCQ—as we say in my restaurant kitchens—has become a Tex-Mex restaurant tradition as well as a frequent dish for parties and football watching. It isn't something I grew up with, however. *Queso* is definitely more Tex than Mex and was likely created in restaurant, not home, kitchens.

Cheese snobs, listen up: Velveeta is a must for making good *queso* because it melts easily and maintains a creamy texture. I add some cheddar as well to boost the cheese flavor. In my opinion, Velveeta has gotten a bit of a bad rap. There's nothing fake about it. Velveeta is cheese! It is processed so that it melts at a lower temperature to provide a consistent product. CCQ needs Velveeta. No negotiating!

Melt your cheese in a double boiler for the smoothest consistency.   *Makes 4 cups*

8 ounces Velveeta cheese, cut into several chunks for faster melting

2 cups (8 ounces) shredded cheddar cheese

1 cup half-and-half

¾ cup chopped white onion

½ cup chopped green bell pepper

½ cup chopped tomato

1 tablespoon all-purpose flour

¾ cup milk

Fill the bottom of a double boiler with water to the fill line. Place over high heat and bring to a boil. Lower the heat to simmer.

In the top of the double boiler over the hot water, combine the cheeses and half-and-half. Cook, stirring every 3 to 4 minutes, until the cheeses are melted and blended with the half-and-half.

Add the onion, bell pepper, and tomato. Over very low heat, cook, stirring frequently, until the vegetables are tender, about 15 minutes.

In a small bowl, combine the flour and milk using a small whisk, stirring until the flour is dissolved and no lumps remain. Pour through a fine strainer to remove any stubborn lumps. Using the whisk, briskly blend the flour and milk mixture into the cheese.

Over very low heat, continue to cook for about 30 minutes, stirring frequently until the sauce thickens. Check the water in the bottom of the double boiler to make sure it does not boil away. Replenish as needed. Maintain a low simmer.

Serve hot. Refrigerate any leftovers. Gently microwave on reheat (50 percent power), stirring frequently, for about 1 minute.

Variations: Add 1 cup Rio Grand Ground Beef (page 44), Fajita Meat (page 108), or *Rajas Poblanos* (page 170), or ½ cup chopped seeded jalapeños.

Sylvia's Enchilada Kitchen Nachos

Nachos are a Tex-Mex restaurant creation. Food lore has it that a restaurant server in Piedras Negras, across the border from Eagle Pass, Texas, created nachos. His given name was Ignacio Anaya, but he was known as Nacho. Forever his name has been associated with the dish he created in a pinch for customers who wanted a cocktail snack. His challenge? Nacho couldn't find the cook, so he ingeniously sprinkled shredded cheese on some chips, topped them with pickled jalapeño slices, then popped them in the oven to melt the cheese.

Nachos have grown in complexity since then, with multiple toppings, including beans, taco meat, shredded chicken, grilled beef and chicken fajitas, even grilled shrimp. Guacamole and sour cream are typical garnishes. Often, *pico de gallo* may be part of the plate.

For the best nachos, don't rely on tortilla chips out of a bag. Crisping fresh corn tortillas then spreading with beans, meat, cheese, and jalapeños or whatever you like, before heating in the oven gives you delicious nachos.

Makes 8 servings

½ cup vegetable oil

8 corn tortillas

Topping: 1 cup Refried Beans (page 164), Classic Rio Grande Ground Beef (page 44), *Pollo Guisado* (page 45), Beef or Chicken Fajitas (page 108), and/or Grilled Shrimp (page 114) or any filling(s) of choice, warm

½ cup drained pickled jalapeño slices (optional)

2 cups coarsely shredded cheddar or Monterey Jack cheese

1 cup Fresh Guacamole (page 89) or Picamole (page 92), or 1 avocado, peeled and sliced (see Enchilada Queen Avocado Wisdom, page 90)

½ cup sour cream

Preheat the oven to 425°F.

In a small skillet over medium-high heat, heat the oil until it shimmers. Fry each tortilla in the hot oil for 2 to 3 minutes, turning once. Tortillas should be lightly crisped. Drain briefly on paper towels.

On an ovenproof serving platter or shallow baking pan, arrange the crisped tortillas in a single layer. Spread each crisped tortilla with your favorite topping or toppings. If using beans, begin with them. That will help other toppings stick to the tortillas.

Sprinkle the tortillas and toppings with jalapeño slices (if desired) and cheese.

Bake for 4 to 6 minutes, until the cheese melts.

Before serving, cut each tortilla into four pieces for nachos.

Serve with the garnishes of your choice, including Guacamole (page 89) or sliced avocado and sour cream.

Coctel de Camaron
SHRIMP COCKTAIL

This recipe is popular in Mexico as well as in South Texas. It is light and refreshing and a very popular restaurant appetizer. I recall enjoying it in Matamoros (Brownsville's twin city), and the *ceviche* is very popular at an old-school restaurant, the Vermillion, in Brownsville. Since Brownsville is only twenty miles from the Gulf of Mexico, this seafood dish is a big favorite.

Makes 8 servings

12 ounces shrimp (26 to 30 shrimp), peeled and deveined
Large bowl of ice and water
1 cup ketchup
¾ cup diced white onion
¾ cup diced tomato
¼ cup chopped fresh cilantro leaves
1 teaspoon salt
2 tablespoons fresh orange juice
Juice of 1 lime
1 avocado, chopped

Bring 2 cups water to a boil in a medium saucepan. Add the shrimp. Immediately remove the saucepan from the heat. Let the shrimp poach in the hot water for about 5 minutes, until just firm and barely pink.

Drain the shrimp in a colander. Turn the drained shrimp into the bowl of ice water and let cool for about 10 minutes, until the shrimp is refrigerator cold (about 37°F).

Chop each chilled shrimp into four pieces.

In a medium bowl, combine the ketchup, onion, tomato, cilantro, salt, and orange and lime juices. Stir well. Add the shrimp and stir again.

Serve in chilled parfait glasses. Garnish each serving with chopped avocado.

Ceviche a la Veracruz

Like many Hispanic dishes, *ceviche* has grown tremendously in popularity in recent years. At Sylvia's Enchilada Kitchen, we make it according to this easy-to-prepare recipe. Still it does take a little advance planning. Use the freshest, best-quality fish you can find, and make the *ceviche* as soon as you get home. Shop for a firm white-fleshed ocean fish, such as red snapper, my favorite. Fresh tortilla chips are handy for scooping *ceviche* out of the dish.

Makes 6 servings

3 (7-ounce) very fresh white fish
   fillets such as red snapper,
   sea bass, striped bass,
   grouper, sole, or flounder
1 cup fresh lime juice
¾ cup finely chopped vine-
   ripened tomato, seeds
   removed, rinsed, and drained
1 (3-inch-long) jalapeño,
   minced
½ cup finely chopped white
   onion
½ cup chopped fresh cilantro
1½ teaspoons salt
½ teaspoon dried Mexican
   oregano
½ teaspoon ground cumin
1½ teaspoons pickled jalapeño
   juice
2 ripe avocados (see Enchilada
   Queen Avocado Wisdom,
   page 90), chopped
2 limes, cut into wedges for
   garnish

Cut the fish fillets into ¼-inch pieces. Place in a nonreactive dish and toss with the lime juice. Cover tightly and refrigerate for 6 hours.

In a medium bowl, combine the tomato, jalapeño, onion, cilantro, salt, oregano, and cumin. Set aside for 30 minutes.

Drain the lime juice from the fish and lightly rinse the fish to "stop" the cooking by the acid; drain.

Combine the vegetables and fish. Serve in individual bowls garnished with a few pieces of avocado and a wedge of lime.

Mexican oregano

Mexican oregano is a relative of lemon verbena, whereas Mediterranean oregano is a kind of mint. Native to Mexico, it also grows in Central and South America and is sometimes referred to as Puerto Rican oregano. Although this herb shares the basic pungent flavor of Mediterranean oregano, it also has notes of citrus and mild licorice. Mexican oregano is almost always used in the dried form. If you need to substitute, try dried marjoram or lemon verbena. If you need to use Mediterranean oregano, use a little less.

Tacos Rancheros
HOMESTYLE TACOS

In South Texas, tacos made with corn tortillas are prepared by lightly frying or grilling the corn tortillas. The tacos are slightly crispy on the outside but soft enough to fold, unlike the industrial-strength hard taco shells found in many fast-food outlets, Tex-Mex restaurants, and on grocery-store shelves. Taco shells that crumble like chips aren't what I grew up on. And they're not the kind I serve. My *Tacos Rancheros* are authentic *frontera*-style tacos.

When making these at home, simplify serving by setting up a "taco bar" with the grilled corn tortillas, beef and/or chicken filling, shredded lettuce, chopped tomato, avocado slices, and salsas. Set this up before you start crisping the tortillas for filling.

Your family will love these delicious homey tacos as much as my children and friends do. In the restaurant, *Tacos Rancheros* are comfort food for South Texans. They also make a great starter or side to serve with enchiladas. Figure on each diner eating at least two and maybe three tacos if tacos are the main course.

Makes 6 to 8 servings

Special Equipment

- Heavy cast-iron *comal* or griddle
- Pastry brush

18 to 24 corn tortillas
½ cup vegetable oil or melted unsalted butter, or a combination
4 cups Rio Grande Ground Beef (page 44) or *Pollo Guisado* (page 45), warm
2 cups shredded iceberg lettuce, cut into 2-inch lengths
1½ cups chopped tomatoes
2 to 3 cups shredded cheddar cheese, as needed
2 to 3 large avocados, cut into 8 slices

Preheat a *comal* or griddle over medium-high heat. The *comal* is ready when water sprinkled on the hot surface "dances." The temperature should be around 400°F.

Using a pastry brush, lightly coat one side of a corn tortilla with oil or melted butter. Place oiled side down on the hot *comal*. Brush the top side of the tortilla with the oil or melted butter.

Using a nonstick spatula, fold the tortilla in half and cook for 2 to 3 minutes. Flip the folded tortilla and cook the other side for another 2 to 3 minutes. The folded tortilla should be slightly golden and slightly crispy on the outside.

Repeat this process for the desired number of tacos. Once you get the hang of it, cook as many tortillas as will fit on the *comal* at one time. Place them on a platter and cover loosely with a towel or foil until you finish grilling the rest of the tortillas. Keep warm in 225°F oven until all the taco shells have been prepared.

Fill each taco with 2 tablespoons of the beef or chicken. Garnish each as desired or let guests fill and garnish to their taste. Fold over to eat.

Gulf Coast Fish Tacos

Fish tacos aren't traditional in South Texas, but I developed my own version in response to customers' many requests. Fish tacos were popularized in Southern California by entrepreneur Ralph Rubio, who loved the tacos he got from beach vendors in Baja California, Mexico. Since the 1980s, fish tacos have been a beloved addition to the "Mexican food" repertoire.

Seasoned *frontera*-style, fried or grilled fish fill my tacos. Use your favorite fish or what's seasonally available, including red snapper, mahi mahi, trout, halibut, catfish, or tilapia. For tacos, less expensive fish is just fine as long as it is fresh. Given that fish tacos were originally cheap beach snacks from vendors, shellfish was seldom used as it wasn't economical enough.

We use fresh handmade Corn Tortillas and garnish with Picamole, my signature chopped avocado and *pico de gallo* combination. Also, Creamy Sauce for Fish Tacos leans to the healthy side with yogurt making up half of the recipe.

When preparing fish tacos, ready the Creamy Sauce and Picamole before grilling or frying the fish. Heat the tortillas last.

Makes 8 servings

8 handmade fresh corn tortillas (page 13) or store-bought white corn tortillas
4 (7- to 9-ounce) white fish filets, Grilled (page 104) or Fried (page 105)
Creamy Sauce for Fish Tacos (see page 104)
Picamole (page 92)
Optional garnishes: shredded cabbage, diced red onion, shredded iceberg or romaine lettuce, diced tomato, *Frontera Pico de Gallo* (page 86)

Prepare the fresh corn tortillas (page 13) and set aside in a tortilla warmer or wrap in a dish towel to keep warm until it is time to assemble the tacos.

If using store-bought tortillas, preheat a *comal* or griddle over medium-high heat. The *comal* is ready when water sprinkled on the hot surface "dances." The temperature should be around 400°F.

Using a nonstick spatula, place tortillas on the hot *comal* and cook on one side until the tortillas puff slightly. Turn and cook to heat through. Stack the hot tortillas in a medium bowl lined with a dish towel or in tortilla warmer.

Repeat until all the tortillas are heated. Fill each warm corn tortilla with ¼ cup of the fish and 2 tablespoons each of Creamy Sauce and Picamole.

Garnish each as desired or let guests fill and garnish to their taste.

Grilled Fish for Tacos

Fish for tacos tastes really wonderful when grilled over hot coals. But you can also pan-cook fish on top of the stove on a griddle or in a heavy skillet.

Makes 8 servings

4 (7- to 9-ounce) skinless white fish fillets, such as red snapper, mahi mahi, trout, halibut, catfish, or tilapia

1 tablespoon Enchilada Queen Seasoning Blend (page 22), or to taste

¼ cup melted unsalted butter, vegetable oil, or a combination

Light a wood or hardwood charcoal fire at least 30 minutes before you are ready to cook. Coals are ready when covered with a light coating of gray ash. Or preheat gas grill to medium-high for 30 minutes. If cooking on the stovetop, preheat a griddle or heavy skillet over medium-high heat.

Sprinkle the seasoning blend evenly on both sides of the fish fillets.

When ready to cook, rub charcoal grill surface lightly with oil. If using a griddle or skillet, lightly butter the griddle or skillet.

Place the fish over the heat. Grill or griddle for 2 to 3 minutes on each side. Fish is done when it pulls apart easily when probed with a fork.

Cut the fish fillets into bite-size pieces; keep warm.

Creamy Sauce for Fish Tacos

Makes 1½ cups

½ cup mayonnaise
½ cup plain yogurt
½ cup ketchup
¼ teaspoon garlic powder
¼ teaspoon salt

In a small bowl, combine all the ingredients, blending well. Refrigerate in a covered container until ready to serve.

Fried Fish for Tacos

4 (7- to 9-ounce) skinless white fish fillets, such as red snapper, mahi mahi, trout, halibut, catfish, or tilapia

1 quart vegetable oil for deep-fryer, or 1-inch-deep oil in a heavy skillet

2 medium eggs, beaten until frothy

½ teaspoon salt

1½ cups cornmeal (regular cornmeal, not *masa harina*)

2 tablespoons Enchilada Queen Seasoning Blend (page 22)

Rinse the fish fillets with cold water and pat dry with a paper towel.

In a deep-fryer, heat the oil to 350°F. In a skillet, use enough oil to come up 1 inch on the inside of the skillet and heat to 350°F.

In a small bowl, whisk together the beaten eggs and salt. Set aside.

Combine the cornmeal with the seasoning blend on a flat plate or pie plate, mixing well.

Dip the fish fillets in the beaten eggs, allowing excess to drip off. Then place the fish fillets in the seasoned cornmeal, turning to coat both sides. Set aside until the oil is hot.

When the oil reaches 350°F, fry the fish fillets, in batches, turning once, until golden brown, 3 to 5 minutes total. Remove to paper towels to drain briefly until all pieces are cooked.

Cut the fish fillets into bite-size pieces; keep warm.

Flautas Rio Grande

Flauta means "flute." That's what these stuffed and rolled then fried tortillas look like, and they play a very sweet song on the plate. Stuffed with chicken, *flautas* are traditionally served with guacamole, sour cream, and salsa. Most of the time, they are served as an appetizer but, like tacos, can easily become the main event. *Flautas* hold up really well and can be made an hour or so ahead of time.

Makes 18 flautas

1½ cups vegetable oil

18 corn tortillas, softened (see below)

2 cups *Pollo Guisado* (page 45), heated through and drained

Toothpicks for securing rolled *flautas*

Sour cream

Fresh Guacamole (page 89)

Enchilada Queen Avocado Salsa Dip (page 91)

In a deep-fryer, Dutch oven or deep skillet, heat the oil to 350°F.

While the oil is heating, place one softened tortilla on a flat work surface. Spoon 1 rounded tablespoon of the chicken down the center. Roll the tortilla tightly, to about ½ inch in diameter. Secure with toothpick(s). Repeat until all tortillas are rolled.

For quicker and easier frying, use toothpicks to "pin" two *flautas* together by running toothpicks through the *flautas* horizontally. Make sure you secure the edge of the tortilla so it doesn't unroll. They are easier to handle this way and less likely to unroll and spill their filling.

When the oil is hot, working in batches, carefully lower *flautas* into the hot oil. Fry for about 2 minutes, until crispy and golden brown. Remove to paper towels to drain. Repeat until all the *flautas* have been fried.

Keep warm in a 225°F oven.

Serve with sour cream, Guacamole, and Avocado Salsa Dip for dipping.

To soften tortillas for *flautas*

In small skillet, heat ½ inch vegetable oil over medium heat until it shimmers, about 300°F. Use a nonstick spatula to slide a tortilla into the oil and cook for about 3 to 5 seconds, or just until pliable. Lift the tortilla and drain off excess oil. Remove the tortilla to a plate. Repeat to soften all tortillas, stacking them as you go. Allow the tortillas to cool for 15 to 20 minutes before rolling flautas.

CHAPTER 6

A LA PARILLA

Border Grilling

Grilling is an important part of South Texas cuisine; mesquite is the firewood of choice. That's because in the many arid parts of this region, mesquite trees are about the only trees that can grow. They thrive in the hot climate and can choke out other, less hearty trees. Mesquite trees range in size from what look like scrawny bushes to respectable trees. Farmers usually consider them weeds on steroids. Ranchers often see them as a fodder of last resort for hungry cattle and goats. Cooks see mesquite as flavor and fire.

Game birds like quail and *cabrito* (baby goat) are South Texas favorites grilled over mesquite. Beef fajitas are, however, the signature grilled meat dish of my home region.

Fajitas are thought to have originated with ranch hands cooking skirt steak (then a throw-away cut) over an open fire while out on the range of South Texas ranches. *Vaqueros* grilled the onions, peppers, and meat over mesquite wood. Hot-off-the-grill skirt steak was cut into thin strips before being wrapped inside a warm flour tortilla. That's a basic fajita. The word in Spanish literally means "little belt."

Houston restaurateur Mama Ninfa (Ninfa Rodriguez Laurenzo) was the queen of fajitas. She is generally credited with popularizing fajitas, beginning with her original Navigation Street restaurant in the early 1970s. The typical restaurant presentation includes sour cream, *pico de gallo*, and guacamole to dress up the plate that, along with strips of grilled beef, also includes grilled green bell peppers and onions. Please note: Mama Ninfa grew up in the Lower River Grande Valley city of Harlingen. She knew the culinary culture in this part of Texas as well as anyone.

When I see a waiter rushing to a table with beef fajitas sizzling on a hot, hot, hot cast-iron griddle, I cringe. That's because I know those fajitas will be overcooked. That's what happens when you put grilled pieces of thin sliced skirt steak on a hot metal surface: the meat keeps cooking. While a sizzling platter is good restaurant theater, it destroys the dish. That's why, at my restaurants, you don't get fajitas on a sizzling hot platter. They come off the grill cooked medium, a rosy pink when sliced. We like to serve them that way . . . with all the fixings.

Frontera Beef (or Chicken) Fajitas

I prefer fajitas cooked over mesquite wood or hardwood charcoal with soaked mesquite chips for smoky flavoring. A gas grill will work, too. For optimum flavor and tenderness, marinate the skirt steaks for 8 hours or overnight.

My marinade enhances the flavor of beef, as well as tenderizes it. Too many fajita marinades overwhelm, even destroy the flavor of the meat. That is a particular risk with the use of liquid smoke to impart smoke flavor. First of all, if you are grilling fajitas over wood or charcoal, the meat will taste smoky. If you aren't grilling over an open fire, don't try to simulate the flavor by adding liquid smoke with its chemical taste to the marinade. Fajitas, with the right marinade, are delicious whether broiled or grilled.

Technically, fajitas aren't chicken. But chicken breast cooked fajita-style has become an in-demand variation on fajitas so I've given up on the semantic argument.

Before grilling, ready your desired garnishes: grilled onions and peppers, guacamole, flour tortillas, *pico de gallo*, and salsa.

Makes 6 servings

Special Equipment

- Charcoal or gas grill
- Heatproof gloves for handling grill equipment
- Mesquite chips or hardwood mesquite charcoal

3½ pounds skirt steak, or
   3 pounds boneless, skinless
   chicken breasts
16 garlic cloves, smashed
2 cups coarsely chopped white
   onions
2½ teaspoons salt
Vegetable oil
1 cup soy sauce mixed with
   ½ cup water
Enchilada Queen Seasoning
   Blend (page 22), as needed
(continued)

Trim any excess fat from the beef or chicken. Using a meat-tenderizing mallet, pound the skirt steaks using the small-pointed side. Set aside.

In a blender jar or work bowl of a food processor, combine the garlic, onion, and 1½ cups water. Process on high speed for at least 30 seconds, until the garlic and onions virtually dissolve.

Transfer the processed garlic and onion with their liquid to a large pitcher. Add the salt and 6 cups water. Stir to dissolve the salt.

Place the skirt steaks or chicken breasts in a shallow nonreactive pan or large plastic bag with zipper seal. Pour the garlic marinade over the meat. Cover or seal; marinate for at least 8 hours in the refrigerator.

Remove the meat from the refrigerator. Drain and discard the marinade. Let the meat sit at room temperature for up to 1 hour.

Meanwhile, light a wood or hardwood charcoal fire at least 30 minutes before you are ready to cook. Coals are ready when

12 warm flour tortillas (page 15)
Garnishes: *Frontera* Grilled
  Onions and Peppers
  (page 168), Fresh Guacamole
  (page 89), *Frontera Pico de
  Gallo* (page 86), *Salsa de Mesa*
  (page 85), and sour cream

covered with a light coating of gray ash. Or preheat a gas grill to medium-high for 30 minutes.

When ready to cook, rub the grill surface lightly with oil. Place the skirt steaks or chicken breasts over the fire in the center of the grill. The heat should be high enough to sear the surface of the meat or chicken when it touches the hot grill.

Brush all sides lightly with the soy sauce and water mixture and lightly sprinkle seasoning blend over all sides of the skirt steaks or chicken. Cook for about 4 minutes on each side for beef fajitas cooked to medium internal temperature. Grill fajitas for about 2 minutes longer if medium-well fajitas are desired. Grill chicken for 6 to 7 minutes per side or until the juices run clear.

Let the meat or chicken rest for about 5 minutes before cutting across the grain into thin strips; trim strips to about 2 inches long.

Serve with warm flour tortillas and garnishes of choice.

Carne Asada
GRILLED STEAK

Using the same marinade for steaks as for fajitas gives great results. It is particularly flavorful on skirt steak, served not as strips, but as a single-serving steak. I also enjoy it on flank steak or a New York strip. Poblano Grits (page 169) are a great go-with.
Makes 4 servings

4 (4- to 6-ounce) skirt, flank, or New York strip steaks
8 garlic cloves, smashed
1 cup coarsely chopped white onion
½ teaspoon salt
Vegetable oil
½ cup soy sauce mixed with ¼ cup water
Enchilada Queen Seasoning Blend (page 22), as needed
Frontera Grilled Onions and Peppers (page 168)

Rinse the steaks and pat dry.

In a blender jar or work bowl of a food processor, combine the garlic, onion, and ¾ cup water. Process on high speed for at least 20 seconds, until the garlic and onion virtually dissolve.

Transfer the pureed garlic and onion with their liquid to a large measuring cup. Add the salt and 2¾ cups water. Stir to dissolve the salt.

Place the steaks in a shallow nonreactive pan or large plastic bag with zipper seal. Pour the garlic marinade over the meat. Cover or seal; marinate for 2 to 4 hours in the refrigerator.

Remove the meat from the refrigerator. Drain and discard the marinade. Let the meat sit at room temperature for up to 1 hour.

Meanwhile, light a wood or hardwood charcoal fire at least 30 minutes before you are ready to cook. Coals are ready when covered with a light coating of gray ash. Or preheat a gas grill to medium-high for 30 minutes.

When ready to cook, rub the grill surface lightly with oil. Place the steaks over the fire in the center of the grill. The heat should be high enough to sear the surface of the meat when it touches the hot grill.

Brush lightly with the soy sauce and water mixture and lightly sprinkle the seasoning blend over the steaks. Immediately turn and brush with the soy sauce and water mixture and season with the seasoning blend. Cook for 3 to 4 minutes on each side for medium-rare internal temperature. Adjust the cooking time based on the thickness of the steaks and desired degree of doneness.

Serve with *Frontera* Grilled Onions and Peppers.

Red Wine Garlic Butter

Makes about 2¼ cups

¼ cup vegetable oil
4 garlic cloves, smashed
1 cup (2 sticks) unsalted butter
½ cup dry red wine
½ cup Worcestershire sauce
1½ tablespoons fresh lemon juice

In a small skillet over medium heat, warm the oil until it shimmers. Stir in the garlic and cook until browned, about 2 to 3 minutes.

Reduce the heat. Add the butter, stirring until melted. Stir in the wine, Worcestershire sauce, and lemon juice. Simmer for 5 minutes. Set aside off the heat until ready to use.

Red-hot mesquite fire for grilling at Sylvia's Enchilada Kitchen restaurant.

Huchinango a la Veracruzana
RED SNAPPER VERACRUZ

Mesquite-grilled seafood represents a beautiful pairing of pungent mesquite smoke and the delicate flavor of fish and shrimp. Enchilada Queen Seasoning Blend plus Red Wine Garlic Butter (or Lime, Garlic, and White Wine Butter, page 23) enhance this combination.

This grilling technique may be used for any white fish fillet, including mahi mahi, trout, halibut, catfish, or tilapia, but fish from the Gulf of Mexico, such as red snapper or redfish, are my fish of choice. Of course, fish may be pan-cooked as well. Grilled fish goes particularly well with Arroz Verde (page 162).

This is a classic combination from the coastal city of Veracruz. Red snapper is abundant in the Gulf of Mexico and a prized game fish as well. *Salsa Veracruzana* (page 36) is the traditional pairing. To develop this recipe, I traveled to this beautiful region of Mexico and dined at various local restaurants recommended for their seafood. Great way to research a recipe!

Makes 8 servings

8 (6- to 7-ounce) skinless red snapper fillets
Red Wine Garlic Butter (see page 112)
Enchilada Queen Seasoning Blend (page 22), as needed
Vegetable oil or unsalted butter
Salsa Veracruzana (page 36)

Light a wood or hardwood charcoal fire at least 30 minutes before you are ready to cook. Coals are ready when covered with a light coating of gray ash. Or preheat a gas grill to medium for 30 minutes. If cooking on the stovetop, preheat a griddle or heavy skillet over medium-high heat.

Rinse the fish fillets with cool water. Pat dry with a paper towel.

Brush the fish on both sides with the Red Wine Garlic Butter. Sprinkle seasoning blend evenly on both sides.

When ready to cook, rub the grill surface lightly with oil. If using a griddle or skillet, lightly butter the surface.

Place the fish over the heat. Grill or griddle for 2 to 3 minutes on each side, depending on thickness. Turn once. Fish is done when it pulls apart easily when probed with a fork. Brush the fish again with Red Wine Garlic Butter.

Serve immediately with *Salsa Veracruzana*.

Mesquite Grilled Shrimp

On the Texas Gulf Coast, Rockport is a small beach town and fishing village known for its shrimp fleet and artists' colony. It is a favorite Texas vacation destination and a charming spot that draws snowbirds in the winter and sun worshippers in the summer.

Giant Rockport shrimp are amazing when cooked over mesquite wood or hardwood charcoal with soaked mesquite chips for smoke flavoring. When grilling shrimp, the bigger the better, because they don't overcook as easily. If you prefer, you may use a griddle or heavy skillet to cook stovetop, but there's no mesquite flavor that way.

Serve Mesquite Grilled Shrimp over *Frontera* Grilled Onions and Peppers. This shrimp also goes well with *Pico de Gallo* (page 86), Guacamole (page 89), rice, beans, and corn tortillas.

Makes 8 servings

4 pounds colossal-size (U-12, no more than 12 shrimp per pound) Gulf shrimp, peeled and deveined
Enchilada Queen Lime, Garlic, and White Wine Butter (page 23)
Enchilada Queen Seasoning Blend (page 22)
Vegetable oil or unsalted butter
***Frontera* Grilled Onions and Peppers (page 168)**

Light a wood or hardwood charcoal fire at least 30 minutes before you are ready to cook. Coals are ready when covered with a light coating of gray ash. Or preheat a gas grill to medium-high. If cooking on the stovetop, preheat a griddle or heavy skillet over medium-high heat.

Rinse the shrimp with cool water. Pat dry with a paper towel.

Brush the shrimp on all sides with the Lime, Garlic, and White Wine Butter. Sprinkle seasoning blend evenly on all sides of the shrimp.

When ready to cook, rub the grill surface lightly with oil. If using a griddle or skillet, lightly butter the griddle or skillet.

Place the shrimp over the heat. Grill or griddle for 2 to 3 minutes on each side, depending on the size of the shrimp. Turn once. Shrimp is done when it turns pink and the flesh becomes firm. Brush the shrimp again with Lime, Garlic, and White Wine Butter.

Serve immediately over *Frontera* Grilled Onions and Peppers (page 168).

Frontera Cabrito
MESQUITE-ROASTED BABY GOAT

Cabrito is a very popular special-occasion dish along the Texas-Mexico border. It is served at weddings, for example. Nothing says "fiesta!" more than *cabrito*. Before I added this dish to my menu, I traveled to Monterrey to eat at all the famous *cabrito* restaurants in that city. The basic preparation is the same: season whole milk-fed baby goats. Then grill the butterflied carcass over hot charcoal. At my restaurants, we cook *cabrito* over mesquite wood, since that's what we burn twelve hours a day.

It took several months to develop our technique, using a brine to ensure both tenderness and flavor. Shop around to find a source for milk-fed baby goat that's no more than 10 pounds. Goats this small are a little harder to find, but make the best *cabrito*.

I suggest marinating *cabrito* in an ice chest or cooler. Keep cool with freezer blocks; melting ice will dilute the brine. Have several freezer blocks ready so you can switch them out. Wash them before refreezing.

You will need a large grill and large roasting pan to cook a whole butterflied *cabrito*. The carcass will measure about 18 inches wide and 2 feet from front to back legs. Or you may ask a butcher to cut the carcass into quarters for easier handling.

Cabrito is often eaten shredded like smoked pork shoulder. It is delicious when served wrapped in fresh corn tortillas, with Charro Beans, sliced avocado, chopped fresh onions, and cilantro.

Makes 8 servings

1 (10-pound) *cabrito*, whole butterflied carcass or cut into quarters
Sylvia's Brine (page 24)
½ cup corn oil
Enchilada Queen Seasoning Blend (page 22), as needed
For serving: Corn Tortillas (page 13), Charro Beans (page 166), sliced avocados, diced onions, and chopped fresh cilantro

To brine the *cabrito*, place it in a cooler. Pour the brine over the *cabrito*. Keep cool with clean, hard frozen freezer blocks, changing them frequently so that the *cabrito* doesn't go over 37°F. Brine for 6 hours.

Drain the brine from the *cabrito* and discard the brine.

Rub the *cabrito* all over with oil. Season generously on all sides with seasoning blend.

Cover and allow the *cabrito* to rest for about 1 hour.

Meanwhile, light a wood or hardwood charcoal fire at least 30 minutes before you are ready to cook. Coals are ready when covered with a light coating of gray ash. Or preheat a gas grill to medium-high. *(continued)*

Frontera Cabrito (continued)

When ready to cook, rub the grill surface lightly with oil.

Place the *cabrito* on the preheated grill and cook for 8 to 10 minutes on each side.

Meanwhile, preheat the oven to 325°F.

Remove the *cabrito* to a roasting pan and cover tightly with foil. Place in the oven, or return the roasting pan to the grill and position it away from direct heat and lower the grill lid. Roast for 2 to 2½ hours, until very tender and the meat is easy to shred.

Set the *cabrito* aside off the heat for 20 minutes to cool. Pull meat in shreds from bones and keep warm.

Serve shredded *cabrito* with tortillas, beans, avocados, onions, and cilantro.

Sylvia Casares gazes at a bend in the Rio Grand River on D. J. Lema's Ranch at Palmito Hill, the southernmost ranch in Texas. *Cabrito,* page 115, on the grill in foreground.

Garlic Butter for Basting Quail

Makes 1 cup

1 cup (2 sticks) unsalted butter
3 garlic cloves, minced
½ teaspoon salt

In a small saucepan over medium heat, combine all the ingredients. Stir and cook for 2 to 3 minutes. Cool slightly or to room temperature. Refrigerate any leftovers.

Grilled South Texas Ranch Quail

Hebronville is a small border town in the heart of South Texas quail country. The region is famed for the wild quail that run through the scrub brush. These small game birds are quite the delicacy. Thank goodness for farm-raised quail. That makes these delicious birds much easier to come by. If quail are not split down the breast, ask the butcher to butterfly and flatten them for grilling.

Brined for flavor and to retain their juices, grilled quail make a wonderful dinner served on a bed of *Frontera* Grilled Onions and Peppers (page 168), with Charro Beans (page 166) and Poblano Grits (page 169). *Makes 6 servings*

12 farm-raised quail, split down
    the breast and pressed to lay
    flat on the grill
Sylvia's Brine (page 24)
Enchilada Queen Seasoning
    Blend (page 22), as needed
Vegetable oil
Garlic Butter for Basting Quail
    (see page 118)

Rinse the quail. Place in plastic bags with zip seals or in a large shallow nonreactive pan. Pour the brine over the quail, seal or cover tightly, and refrigerate for 2 to 4 hours.

Drain the brine from the quail and discard the brine. Pat the quail dry with a paper towel.

Season the quail evenly on both sides with seasoning blend. Cover and allow to rest for about 1 hour.

Meanwhile, light a wood or hardwood charcoal fire at least 30 minutes before you are ready to cook. Coals are ready when covered with a light coating of gray ash. Or preheat a gas grill to medium-high. When ready to cook, rub the grill surface lightly with oil.

Place the quail on the preheated grill and cook for 3 to 5 minutes. Baste with Garlic Butter. Turn and cook for 3 to 5 more minutes, basting again.

Remove the quail to a flat roasting pan. Baste once more with Garlic Butter. Cover tightly with foil and set aside off the heat for about 10 minutes. Preheat the oven to 325°F. Test the quail for doneness: The juices should run clear when the thigh is pierced with a fork. If not quite done, place the covered roasting pan in the oven for 10 minutes. Serve immediately.

CHAPTER 7

ENCHILADA QUEEN HOMESTYLE

Soups and Stews, Family Dishes, and "Mexican Breakfast"

Many diners are introduced to Tex-Mex dishes in restaurants. Dishes such as *chile con queso*, chips and salsa, loaded nachos, crispy tacos, and fancy enchiladas. Customers love them and, for many, the dishes epitomize Tex-Mex. These are the dishes that often make up Tex-Mex combo plates and come immediately to mind when many a Texan—especially one who didn't grow up along the border—craves "some Mexican food."

There is, however, another kind of food that is traditional along *la frontera*. It is homestyle cooking—that is, Mom or comfort food. Some dishes of this genre overlap on restaurant menus, of course, especially breakfast dishes such as *migas*, and tamales, eaten in almost every home as part of the Christmas holiday festivities. Family *tamaladas*—tamale-making parties—are traditional. When I was a kid, we made the tamales with Mamá Grande. As we got older and my mother got busier, it became more practical to buy tamales to eat on Christmas Eve. Pretty much everyone eats tamales on Christmas Eve. Making tamales to sell for the

holiday is a time-honored cottage industry in small towns along the border.

Many other dishes that I and a lot of other South Texas kids grew up eating are seldom made anywhere but home kitchens. Yes, some restaurants serve some of these dishes. I offer a few at mine. *Sopa de fideo*, a Tex-Mex version of SpaghettiOs, is one. *Arroz con pollo* (chicken with rice) is another. These are the kinds of dishes my mother and lots of moms all over the region prepared on a daily basis. They taste great while being very economical. We ate *arroz con pollo* once a week. Also a skillet dish of *calabacitas* with chicken or pork, *caldo*, and, of course, *fideo*.

As adults we feel sentimental when we cook and eat the foods we grew up on. They remind us of home. The aromas and flavors are comforting. We think of simpler times; days and evenings when "What's for dinner?" wasn't our problem. It was what we looked forward to, especially when dinner was one of our favorite dishes. I get homesick just thinking about many of the recipes in this chapter. I love to make them for the nostalgia they evoke. I hope my (now grown up) children feel the same way about these dishes because they were the comfort food I prepared for them at home when they were young.

Soups and stews are a key category of comfort food, especially dishes like *carne guisada* (beef stew), *caldo de res* (beef vegetable soup), and tortilla soup. Many of these are frequently found in restaurants as well, where they are just as comforting.

Soups and Stews

Typically, Rio Grande–style meals in a bowl are richly flavored, though the ingredients may be modest. The deep flavor of chiles and savory herbs used in braised meats and poultry go a long way to making dishes taste like a million bucks when they only cost a few dollars. And these dishes will fill up growing teens and hardworking adults. They provide a ton of nutrition for the cost. These are simple dishes—nothing exotic, but when done right, they are so flavorful, packed with the kinds of flavors I grew up with.

I make two versions of tortilla soup. My favorite is the first one. Though it has tomato sauce in it, the broth is very lightly tinged, almost clear like plain chicken stock. To enrich the broth, I add a touch of chicken bouillon. I love the mix of fresh vegetables in this soup; tomatoes, potatoes, carrots, onion, and *calabacitas*. Note: Add potatoes last and cook just until fork tender so they don't fall apart. I garnish it with what I call "Tortilla Croutons," crispy squares of tortillas. It's okay to use tortilla chips out of a bag.

About Knorr chicken bouillon

Notice that many soup and sauce dishes that use chicken broth call for Knorr chicken bouillon as a flavor booster. This product is in almost every South Texas and Mexican kitchen that I've ever been in. I grew up using it but, through the years, I've had second thoughts, fearing other professionals or gourmet diners would object because bouillon wouldn't be considered "pure" or authentic. After I found gallon containers of Knorr for sale in a village *mercado* south of Mexico City, I changed my mind. If this product is available that remotely, it must be good. I realized that that many cooks can't be wrong. So I thought, "Okay, I'm off the hook!" I can use this product so beloved in Latin kitchens. In fact, Knorr has a whole line of "Latin Flavors," all widely used in Mexico and along the border.

Enchilada Queen Tortilla Soup

If chicken noodle soup is "Jewish penicillin," this is "Tex-Mex penicillin." I make this for someone I love who has a bad cold or flu. But you don't have to feel bad to feel good eating it.

Makes 6 servings

5 cups chicken stock (page 18)

1½ teaspoons salt

1 tablespoon chicken base or Knorr chicken bouillon

2 teaspoons Tex-Mex Holy Trinity Spice Paste (page 20)

2 cups coarsely chopped tomatoes

1½ cups chopped yellow onions

2 carrots, peeled and cut into ½-inch pieces, about 1½ cups

2 *calabacitas* (Mexican squash) or zucchini, unpeeled and cut into ½-inch pieces, about 2 cups

1 stalk celery, sliced, about ¾ cup

1 bay leaf

¼ cup tomato sauce

4 red potatoes, cut into 1-inch pieces, about 2 cups

Crispy Tortilla "Croutons" (see below), or ¼ cup crumbled tortilla chips per bowl

1½ cups shredded Chihuahua or Monterey Jack cheese

1 avocado (see Enchilada Queen Avocado Wisdom, page 90), coarsely chopped

In a large saucepan, Dutch oven, or stockpot over high heat, combine the broth, salt, chicken base, and Holy Trinity. When the broth begins to boil, add the tomatoes, onions, carrots, *calabacitas*, celery, bay leaf, and tomato sauce. Reduce the heat and simmer for 5 minutes.

Add the potatoes and simmer for another 7 to 10 minutes, or until the potatoes are easily pierced with a fork but not falling apart.

If you are not serving the soup right away, use a slotted spoon to remove the vegetables from the soup and place in shallow baking pan so the vegetables do not continue to cook and get mushy. When ready to serve, return the vegetables to steaming-hot broth and heat through.

To serve, ladle broth and vegetables into a bowl (or cup). Top each serving with ½ to ⅓ cup Crispy Tortilla "Croutons" and about ¼ cup cheese. Garnish with 4 or 5 chunks of avocado.

Crispy Tortilla "Croutons"

Allow about 1 tortilla per serving of soup. Cut each tortilla into 1-inch squares. In a heavy skillet over medium-high heat, heat 2 cups vegetable oil to 350°F. Line a shallow baking pan with paper towels. Using a slotted spoon or spatula, carefully slide a handful of tortilla squares into the hot oil and fry until light golden and crisp, about 3 minutes. Remove from the oil, allowing excess oil to drain. Transfer to the paper towels to drain.

Caldo de Res
VEGETABLE BEEF SOUP

A rich vegetable soup made with beef shank, *Caldo de Res* is distinguished by big chunks of vegetables, including 2-inch pieces of corn on the cob and several varieties of squash. *Caldo*, as it is known, is usually served with a side of Mexican rice (page 161), half a lime or lemon, and corn tortillas. It is as often eaten for a late breakfast, especially in restaurants on weekends, as it is for lunch anytime.

My mother prepared *caldo* for us especially in cool months, always for lunch. I remember her going to market to buy fresh vegetables for soup. Her *Caldo de Res* is unusual because she added sweet potatoes. You'll find them in this recipe. The sweetness of yams and saltiness of the broth makes me think of my mom. *Makes 10 to 12 servings*

4 pounds beef shank, in pieces about 1 inch long

1 pound beef stew meat, cut into 1-inch pieces

1½ cups chopped onions

1 tablespoon salt

3 tablespoons beef base (Better than Bouillon brand preferred)

1 bay leaf

2 tablespoons Tex-Mex Holy Trinity (page 20)

2 ears of corn, cut into 2-inch lengths

2 cups *calabacitas* or zucchini cut into 1-inch pieces

2 cups unpeeled red or russet potatoes cut into 1-inch pieces

1½ cups tomatoes cut into 1-inch chunks

1 (6-ounce) chayote squash, cut into 1-inch chunks

2 cups thickly sliced celery

2 cups thickly sliced carrots

3 cups coarsely chopped cabbage

1 (4-ounce) sweet potato, peeled or not, sliced 1 inch thick

3 tablespoons tomato sauce

Lime or lemon wedges

Leaves from ½ bunch fresh cilantro

Leaves from 2 stems fresh mint

In a large stockpot or Dutch oven over high heat, combine the beef shank, stew meat, 3 gallons water, the onions, salt, beef base, and bay leaf. Bring to a boil over high heat, then reduce the heat, cover, and simmer for 2 hours, or until the meat is very tender.

Add the Holy Trinity, corn, *calabacitas*, potatoes, tomatoes, chayote, celery, carrots, cabbage, sweet potato, and tomato sauce. Simmer for 15 to 20 minutes, until the potatoes are tender when pierced with a fork.

Set aside off the heat for 15 to 20 minutes before serving.

To serve, ladle the beef and vegetables into large soup bowls with plenty of broth. Garnish each with a lemon wedge. Tear cilantro and mint leaves into the hot soup just before eating.

La Fondita Tortilla Soup

I adapted this recipe from a soup I had in a small village south of Mexico City, Tepotzlan. It is one of Mexico's *pueblos majicos*, which means "magic towns." "Tepoz," as many of the locals refer to the precious little village, is home to several *fondas* or *fonditas*, very small emporiums—local eateries where families live in the back and make a restaurant in the front of the house. They serve heritage recipes to tourists and weekend visitors from Mexico City who have escaped to enjoy the peace and tranquility of this special place. It was in one of these *fondas* that I first had this soup. Though their town is far from the bright lights and big stores of Mexico City, the cooks in these *fondas*, and the "food courts" of the *mercados* (markets), manage to find and buy large containers of Knorr chicken bouillon. I smiled when I observed the gallon container of this wonderful flavoring for soups. It's a staple in most Mexican and Texas-Mexican pantries. It certainly is in mine.

This soup calls for epazote, a pungent herb common in Mexican cooking. Besides being used for its unique flavor, it is a common ingredient in black bean dishes because epazote contains compounds that reduce intestinal gas, a familiar byproduct of bean consumption. If you can't find epazote in local Hispanic markets, don't sweat it. There's no flavor substitute, but you'll still love this soup, spicier and redder than the recipe that precedes it. And you can always use Beano or a similar product to bypass the gas.

Makes 8 servings

8 (4- to 6-inch) guajillo chiles, stems and seeds removed

1 *chile de árbol*, stem removed (no need to remove seeds)

2 tablespoons vegetable oil

¼ cup chopped white onion

3 garlic cloves, minced, plus 3 whole garlic cloves

3 cups chopped tomatoes

4 corn tortillas, cut into 1-inch pieces

3 cups chicken stock (page 18)

2 teaspoons salt

1½ teaspoons chicken base or Knorr chicken bouillon

(continued)

In a medium saucepan over high heat, combine the dried chiles with 3¼ cups water. Bring to a boil, then reduce the heat and simmer for 15 minutes. Set aside off the heat for 10 minutes.

In a blender jar or work bowl of a food processor, process the chiles and their cooking liquid on low speed for 10 seconds. Increase the speed to high and blend for 45 seconds, or until smooth. Pour the mixture through a fine strainer into a medium bowl. Discard the solids. You should have 3 cups puree. Set aside.

In the same saucepan over medium-high heat, heat the oil until it shimmers. Add the onion; cook and stir for 3 to 4 minutes. Add the minced garlic and cook until the onion is soft but not brown, about 2 to 3 minutes.

(continued)

2 to 3 sprigs fresh or dried epazote (optional)

1 large avocado, chopped (see Enchilada Queen Avocado Wisdom, page 90)

1 cup corn kernels, frozen (thawed) or fresh corn, pan-toasted (page 162)

½ cup chopped fresh cilantro

Crispy Tortilla Strips (see below)

1 cup shredded Chihuahua or Monterey Jack cheese

In a blender jar or work bowl of a food processor, process 2 cups of the tomatoes, the tortillas, and whole garlic cloves on high speed for 30 seconds, or until smooth. Pass through a strainer to remove any solids. Discard the solids.

In a large saucepan over high heat, combine the chile puree, cooked onion and garlic, blended tomato mixture, broth, salt, bouillon, and epazote, if using, and bring to a boil. Reduce the heat and simmer for about 15 minutes. Remove the epazote sprigs and discard. Off the heat, cover the soup and set aside for 10 minutes to let the flavors blend.

To serve, ladle soup into bowls. Garnish with the remaining tomatoes, the avocado, corn, and cilantro. Top with Crispy Tortilla Strips and 2 tablespoons cheese per serving.

Crispy Tortilla Strips

Cut 3 corn tortillas into strips, ½ inch wide and 2 inches long. In a large skillet over high heat, heat 2 cups vegetable oil to 350°F. Fry the tortilla strips in 2 batches, until golden and crispy. Drain on paper towels.

Sylvia's *Caldo de Pollo*
CHICKEN VEGETABLE SOUP

A big pot of chicken soup is another winter kitchen memory for me. My mother made *Caldo de Pollo* more often when it was cold. With big pieces of vegetables like *Caldo de Res*, this is a chicken version without sweet potato. *Caldo de Pollo* is very much home comfort food as well as a restaurant favorite sold to-go or for dining in. It is usually served with a side of Mexican rice (page 161), half a lime or lemon, and corn tortillas.

I also offer a white-meat-only variation of this recipe for those who prefer. Though delicious, the broth isn't as rich without using both white and dark meat chicken. **Makes 8 servings**

2 to 2½ pounds white and dark meat chicken pieces, bone-in and skin-on

2 teaspoons salt

1 cup chopped white onion

½ cup coarsely chopped tomato

2 garlic cloves, smashed

4 teaspoons chicken base or Knorr chicken bouillon

½ cup sliced carrot

½ cup sliced celery

1 ear corn on the cob, cut into 2-inch lengths

½ cup coarsely chopped *calabacita* or zucchini

1 unpeeled red or russet potato, coarsely chopped to make ½ cup

In a large saucepan or stockpot over high heat, combine the chicken pieces, 2 quarts water, and the salt. Bring to a boil, then reduce the heat and simmer for about 25 minutes. Set aside off the heat for 10 minutes.

In a blender jar or work bowl of a food processor, process the onion, tomato, garlic, and ¼ cup water for 20 seconds, or until smooth.

Using a slotted spoon, remove the chicken to a large bowl. When cool enough to handle, pull off skin and tear meat from the bones in small pieces. Discard the skin and bones. Return the chicken meat and any accumulated juices to the pot with the broth.

Place the pot over low heat. Add the chicken base and bring to a simmer. Stir well to dissolve the base.

Stir in the processed onion and tomato mixture, the carrot, celery, and corn; simmer for about 10 minutes.

Add the *calabacita* and potatoes. Simmer for about 10 minutes, just until the potatoes can be pierced easily with a fork. Serve.

White-meat-only option: In a large saucepan or stockpot over high heat, combine 1½ to 2 pounds bone-in, skin-on chicken breast, 2 quarts water, and 1 teaspoon salt. Bring to a boil, then reduce the heat and simmer for about 20 minutes. Proceed as above beginning with step 2.

Sylvia's *Sopa de Fideo*
VERMICELLI SOUP

This homestyle favorite is also very popular with customers and staff at my restaurant, one of the few that serves this traditional dish. Made with thin pasta, *fideo* is a weekday staple in Texas border towns. This recipe brings back some of the most wonderful memories of my mom's cooking. We loved it for lunch or dinner and she always prepared it with chicken pieces so it was wonderfully filling.

Today I love to add *Charro* Beans (page 166) to my *fideo* soup, and it takes me back to my mother's kitchen on 19th Street. I use my mom's recipe—the best, and the version that *frontera* kids dream of when they are far from home. With a tomato sauce base, this comfort food is a Tex-Mex riff on SpaghettiOs but oh-so-much better. My mother made it once a week, typically, for lunch back in the days when dads came home for lunch. She prepared it as a skillet meal with whole pieces of chicken, browned then braised with pasta and veggies.

Many of my customers have learned to love this very special menu item as a new style of thick chicken soup. Others, who grew up eating this for supper once a week as kids like I did, are thrilled to find a restaurant that serves it. This recipe is for when you can't get to Sylvia's Enchilada Kitchen.

In this dish and in Mexican cooking, pasta is usually toasted (lightly browned in the skillet or saucepan) before being stewed with liquid and other ingredients. This is, I believe, unique to Mexican and border cooking, unlike Italian techniques where pasta is usually boiled.

Makes 6 servings

3 tablespoons vegetable oil

1 (5-ounce) box vermicelli pasta

¼ cup chopped white onion

1 cup coarsely chopped tomato

4½ cups chicken stock (page 18)

¼ cup chopped green bell pepper

¼ cup tomato sauce

2 teaspoons Tex-Mex Holy Trinity (page 20)

½ teaspoon salt

1½ to 2 cups shredded cooked chicken (optional)

In a large skillet over medium heat, heat 2 tablespoons of the oil. Add the vermicelli and cook, stirring frequently, until light golden brown. Place the browned pasta in a large saucepan or stockpot.

Using the same skillet over medium heat, add the remaining 1 tablespoon oil and the onion. Cook, stirring occasionally, until the onion is transparent. Set aside off the heat.

In a blender jar or using a mini-chopper, process the chopped tomato with ¼ cup water for about 30 seconds, until smooth.

To the large saucepan or stockpot with the browned pasta, add the broth, onion, processed tomatoes, bell pepper, tomato sauce, Holy Trinity, and salt.

Over high heat, bring to a boil, then reduce the heat, cover, and simmer for 10 minutes. Set aside off the heat, uncovered so the pasta does not overcook, for 5 minutes. Stir in the chicken before serving, if desired.

Crema de Elote con Jaiba
CORN AND CRAB SOUP

I first tasted this soup in Cancun on a culinary tour of Mexico and fell in love. I make it at home with Gulf blue crab as a special treat. It can be made with chicken for everyday meals. Whether made with crab or chicken, this creamy soup is delicious, especially if you love corn as I do.

Makes 8 servings

5 cups frozen corn kernels, thawed, or about 6 ears of corn

2½ cups chicken broth

4 garlic cloves, minced

1¼ cups chopped white onion

1¼ cups chopped celery

¼ cup unsalted butter

¼ cup all-purpose flour

1 cup whole milk

2 cups heavy whipping cream

2 teaspoons chicken base or Knorr chicken bouillon

1 teaspoon salt

¼ teaspoon cayenne pepper (optional)

1 pound fresh lump crabmeat or 2 cups shredded cooked chicken

⅓ cup panko (Japanese-style) bread crumbs

If using frozen corn, place 2½ cups thawed corn and 1 cup broth in a blender jar or work bowl of a food processor. Process for about 30 seconds, until smooth. Repeat to process the remaining corn and 1 cup broth. Pass the corn mixture through a fine strainer to remove remaining solids. Discard the solids. Set the strained corn liquid aside.

If using fresh corn, shuck the corn and remove silk. Cut the cobs in half. In a large saucepan or stockpot over high heat, combine the corn and 3 quarts water; bring to a boil, then reduce the heat and simmer for about 10 minutes. Using a slotted spoon, remove the corn to a large bowl and set aside to cool for about 30 minutes. To speed cooling, place the corn in a large pan of ice water.

When the corn is cool enough to handle, firmly grasp a cob and position it vertically over a large shallow bowl. Using a sharp chef's knife, cut down the length of the cob to remove the kernels. Once all the kernels have been cut from the cobs, you should have about 5 cups.

If using fresh corn, place 2½ cups fresh-cut corn and 1 cup broth in a blender jar or work bowl of a food processor. Process for about 30 seconds, until smooth. Repeat to process the remaining corn and 1 cup broth. Pass the corn mixture through a fine strainer to remove remaining solids. Discard the solids. Set the strained corn liquid aside. *(continued)*

In a blender jar or work bowl of a food processor, process the garlic, onion, and celery with the remaining ½ cup broth for about 1 minute, until smooth. Pass the mixture through a fine strainer; discard any remaining solids. Combine with strained corn liquid.

In large saucepan over medium heat, melt the butter. When the butter is bubbly, whisk in the flour. Stir and cook until the flour turns a very light tan color to make a roux.

Gradually stir in the strained corn liquid.

In a small skillet over medium heat, combine the milk and cream, stirring well to blend. Add the chicken base, ½ teaspoon of the salt, and the cayenne, if using. Stirring frequently, bring to a boil, then immediately reduce the heat and simmer for 15 minutes, stirring every 2 minutes.

In a medium bowl, gently combine the crabmeat with the bread crumbs and the remaining ½ teaspoon salt so the crabmeat does not come apart. To serve, place 2 heaping tablespoons of the crab mixture in the center of a soup bowl. Ladle about ½ cup of the hot soup over the crab, or place crab on top of soup.

If using chicken, omit previous step and stir the shredded chicken into the soup.

Serve immediately.

Puerco Guisada
BRAISED PORK

This version of braised pork has multiple uses. It can be eaten as stew, like *Carne Guisada* (page 134), or used as filling for tamales. Shred the cooked pork for tamales. Cube and crisp it for *guisada*. You may want to halve this recipe if you aren't using it for tamale filling since it makes a large amount.   *Makes 10 servings*

3½ to 4 pounds boneless pork butt, in one piece

2 cups chopped onions

8 garlic cloves, minced (5 for the pork, 3 for the chile sauce)

2 teaspoons salt

8 guajillo chiles, stems and seeds removed

2 *chiles de árbol*, stems removed (no need to remove seeds)

2 teaspoons Tex-Mex Holy Trinity (page 20)

¾ teaspoon dried Mexican oregano

¼ cup vegetable oil (if making stew)

In a large saucepan, Dutch oven, or stockpot over high heat, combine the pork, 2 cups water, 1 cup of the onions, 5 minced garlic cloves, and 1 teaspoon of the salt. Bring to a boil, then lower the heat, cover, and simmer for about 1 hour 30 minutes, until the pork is very tender. Set aside off the heat until the meat is cool enough to handle. For faster cooling, remove the meat from the liquid. (Strain the stock and reserve for preparing tamale *masa*, if making tamales.)

Meanwhile, in a large saucepan over high heat, combine 2½ cups water, the remaining 1 cup onions, the remaining 3 minced garlic cloves, the dried chiles, Holy Trinity, 1 teaspoon salt, and the oregano. Bring to a boil, then reduce the heat and simmer for 15 minutes. Set aside off the heat for 10 to 15 minutes.

In a blender jar or work bowl of a food processor, process the cooked chiles and their liquid for about 10 seconds on low speed, then on high for about 45 seconds, until smooth.

Return the blended chile mixture to the saucepan over low heat. Simmer for about 15 minutes. Set aside off the heat.

When the pork is cool enough to handle:

For tamales, pull pork into shreds, then finely chop, trimming off and discarding excess fat.

For stew, pull the pork into chunks and cut into ¾-inch pieces, trimming off and discarding excess fat. In a large skillet over medium heat, heat the oil to 350°F. Cook the pork pieces for about 5 minutes, until crispy. Remove from the pan with a slotted spoon to drain excess oil.

In a large saucepan, combine the shredded or cubed pork with the chile sauce and use for tamales, or heat through and serve as stew.

Frontera Carne Guisada

BEEF STEW BORDER STYLE

Beef stew, or *Carne Guisada*, is a traditional dish cooked in most border homes at least once a week, especially during the cooler months. The thought of *guisada* simmering in my mother's and grandmother's kitchens makes me hungry. Regardless of the season, *Carne Guisada* is a lunch favorite at Sylvia's Enchilada Kitchen as well, one of the more popular nonenchilada choices.

The pronounced cumin flavor in a typical *Carne Guisada* comes from The Tex-Mex Holy Trinity, a garlic, cumin, and black pepper spice paste. I also add some dried chiles to this dish, thus making it a little different than traditional recipes. *Chiles guajillos* add a smoky heat and brick red color.

This simple stew is eaten many ways: as a stew sometimes with potatoes, a meat sauce with Rio Grande Rice (page 136), a breakfast dish with "Mexican Breakfast" Potatoes (page 148), and with eggs, scrambled plain as well as fried and served on top of the stew. For lunch, *guisada* is usually served with rice, beans, and tortillas.   **Makes 8 servings**

---

3 pounds beef stew meat, cut into ¾-inch pieces

3 (5-inch) guajillo chiles, stems and seeds removed

1 small *chile de árbol*, stem removed (no need to remove seeds)

1 cup chopped white onion

1 cup chopped tomato

½ cup chopped green bell pepper

¼ cup tomato sauce

2 teaspoons Tex-Mex Holy Trinity (page 20)

¼ teaspoon dried Mexican oregano

2 to 3 bay leaves

1½ teaspoons salt

2 tablespoons vegetable oil

2 tablespoons all-purpose flour

1 large russet potato, peeled and cut into ¾-inch pieces (optional)

In a large saucepan over high heat, combine the meat with 4 cups water. Bring to a boil, then reduce the heat and simmer for about 15 minutes. Using a large spoon, skim the frothy material that rises during cooking.

Cover and simmer for 1 hour and 15 minutes.

Meanwhile, in a small saucepan, combine the dried chiles with 1 cup water. Bring to a boil, then reduce the heat and simmer for about 15 minutes; set aside off the heat and let cool to lukewarm.

In a blender jar or work bowl of a food processor, process the lukewarm chiles and their cooking liquid. Process on low speed for about 10 seconds, then on high for about 45 seconds, until the sauce is a smooth brick red.

Pass the blended chiles through a fine strainer to remove any solids. Discard the solids. Reserve ½ cup of the chile liquid.

To the meat in the saucepan, add the onion, tomato, and bell pepper. Stir in the ½ cup chile liquid, the tomato sauce, Holy Trinity, oregano, bay leaves, and salt. Simmer for 20 minutes, or until the meat is fork tender.

Meanwhile, in a small skillet over medium heat, heat the oil. Whisk in the flour and stir until golden tan in color. Set aside off the heat. Add a small amount of liquid from the stew pot and stir to remove any lumps.

When the meat is very tender, stir in the flour mixture. Add the potatoes, if using. Stir occasionally while simmering for another 10 minutes, or until the stew is thickened and the potatoes are tender. Serve immediately.

Rio Grande Valley *Arroz con Pollo*
CHICKEN WITH RICE

Arroz con Pollo is a family skillet dinner, *frontera* style. Chicken with rice is a major comfort food for me and many others who grew up along the border. My grandmother and mother made it for me and my brother. This dish was one of the first things I learned to cook. I made it for my children and taught them how to cook it as well.

Back in the days when chickens were only sold whole, my mother would cut up a chicken into serving pieces to make this dish. She'd cut the entire breast into 4 pieces. Today, when chicken pieces come in packs, use any pieces you like. Dark meat like thighs and drumsticks are more flavorful. If using bone-in, skin-on half breasts, cut each into two same-size pieces. You may also want to try this with 18 drummettes.

When you're in a hurry, use shredded chicken from another recipe or from a supermarket deli roasted chicken.

Important to remember: It's okay to pick up bone-in chicken pieces to eat with your hands. Enjoy as finger-licking good. Use a fork for the rice.

Note that the recipe requires long-grain rice. Short-grain or parboiled—quick-cooking—rice will be gummy and it won't brown properly.

Makes 6 servings

4 tablespoons vegetable oil

12 pieces chicken (legs, thighs, wings, breast quarters), or 18 drummettes, or 2 cups shredded cooked chicken

1½ cups coarsely chopped tomatoes

1 clove garlic

1⅓ cups long-grain white rice

¼ cup chopped white onion

3 tablespoons tomato sauce

2 teaspoons Tex-Mex Holy Trinity (page 20)

1 teaspoon salt

In a large skillet with a lid over medium heat, heat 2 tablespoons of the oil until it shimmers. Add the chicken pieces. Cover and cook for about 20 minutes, turning occasionally, to brown all sides. Remove the chicken and its juices to a shallow pan and keep warm. Omit this step if using shredded cooked chicken.

In a blender jar or work bowl of a food processor, combine the tomatoes, garlic, and ¼ cup water. Process for 20 seconds, or until smooth. Set aside.

After the chicken is brown, in the same large skillet over medium heat, combine the remaining 2 tablespoons oil and the rice. Cook, stirring every minute, until the rice turns a light golden yellow, about 5 minutes.

To the rice in the skillet, carefully stir in the processed tomato mixture, the onion, 2½ cups water, the tomato sauce, Holy Trinity, and salt. Stir well to combine. *(continued)*

If using bone-in chicken, crowd the pieces in a single layer over the rice.

Return the skillet to high heat. Bring the liquid to a boil, then reduce the heat and simmer, covered, for 15 minutes.

Set aside off the heat, covered, for 5 minutes to finish cooking.

If using shredded chicken, stir the chicken into the rice to heat through just before serving.

Chiles Relleños
STUFFED POBLANO PEPPERS

Because *Chiles Relleños* are a lot of work, they are special-occasion dishes when made in home kitchens. The peppers must be blistered in oil, filled, battered, and fried. I offer hands-on *Chile Relleño* lessons at my restaurant and students have a blast.

Large, dark green poblano peppers may be stuffed with a variety of fillings. Besides Monterey Jack cheese, one of the more popular at the restaurants is Rio Grande Ground Beef (page 44). Other fillings often requested include Beef Fajitas (page 108), Tampico Shrimp (page 75), and *Pollo Guisado* (page 45).

Makes 6 servings

Special Equipment

- **2 flat nonstick spatulas for handling the chiles in the skillet**

6 large (6-inch) poblano peppers

4 cups vegetable oil

3 cups shredded Monterey Jack cheese; or 6 tablespoons cheese plus 3 cups Rio Grande Ground Beef (page 44), Beef Fajitas (page 108), *Pollo Guisado* (page 45), or Tampico Shrimp (page 75)

1 cup all-purpose flour

12 large eggs, yolks and whites separated (see "How to Separate Eggs," page 141)

Salsita (page 142; optional)

Rinse the poblano peppers, pat dry with a paper towel, and set aside.

In a large deep skillet over medium-high heat, heat the oil to 350°F.

Place one pepper at a time in the oil, turning to evenly heat all sides. The pepper should be slightly "blistered" and have a whitish skin. Place the pepper on a platter lined with paper towels to absorb grease. Repeat until all the peppers have been blistered in oil. Set the oil aside off the heat to cool.

Using a serrated knife, pull blistered skin from the stem end from each pepper. Using a sharp paring knife, cut a 2-inch opening lengthwise in each, starting at the stem end. Remove most of the seeds.

Carefully stuff each pepper with ½ cup filling. If using meat, shrimp, or chicken filling, mix ½ cup filling with 1 tablespoon cheese for each pepper so the filling sticks together. Do not overstuff the peppers. If the cut edges don't close snugly together, the pepper is too full.

Place the flour in a shallow bowl or pie plate. Roll the stuffed peppers in flour to evenly coat; set aside.

Using an electric mixer and a large bowl, whip the egg whites until stiff peaks form.

(continued)

In a medium bowl, lightly beat the egg yolks. Fold the yolks into the stiffened egg whites and beat very briefly on medium speed until the yolks are well blended and the mixture is a light yellow color. This should only take a few seconds.

Reheat the oil in the skillet over medium-high heat to 350°F. Preheat the oven to 225°F.

When the oil is hot, place one flour-coated poblano in the egg to coat evenly. Pick up the battered pepper by the stem or stem end and gently slide it into the hot oil. If a pepper has a spot with little or no batter, add a little additional batter by dropping enough of the batter on the spot while the pepper is beginning to fry.

Using two flat nonstick spatulas, gently splash hot oil over the top side of the pepper while it is frying. The top side of the batter will begin to firm and turn a very light golden yellow while the batter in the oil is cooking and becoming a beautiful golden brown color.

When the bottom of the pepper has cooked to a golden brown, roll the poblano using both spatulas, and cook the other side. It should be golden brown all over. Place the peppers on a platter lined with paper towels to soak up excess grease. Repeat until all the peppers are battered and fried. Keep warm in the oven.

Serve with *Salsita*, if desired.

How to separate eggs

1. Set up three bowls. Bowl #1 should be a large oil-free bowl reserved for beating egg whites.

2. Bowl #2 should be a medium bowl for egg yolks.

3. Bowl #3 is strictly for receiving the egg white as it separates from the yolk. Even a tiny drop of yolk in the egg white will prevent the batter from stiffening, so be very careful not to break the yolk.

4. To separate, carefully crack the egg shell and gently pull apart. Pour the egg through an egg separator or your fingers, catching the white in bowl #3.

5. The unbroken yolk should remain in the cup of the separator or your palm. If the yolk does not break and contaminate the egg white, transfer the egg white to bowl #1 and repeat until all the eggs are separated. Place yolks in bowl #2. Use as desired.

6. Egg whites in bowl #3 *must* be yolk free in order to stiffen and peak when they are whipped.

Salsita (Little Sauce) for *Chiles Relleños*

This is a simple, fresh sauce to top *Chiles Relleños*. I created it on a whim and my guests love it. You can vary the amount of heat in this recipe by the size of the jalapeño. The secret is fresh garlic.

Makes 3 cups

4 medium tomatoes, cut into
   wedges
½ medium (4-inch) jalapeño
2 garlic cloves, minced
1 teaspoon salt

In a small saucepan over high heat, combine the tomatoes, jalapeño, and 2 cups water. Bring to a boil, then reduce the heat and simmer for 20 minutes. Set aside off the heat to cool for 10 minutes.

In the saucepan, mash the cooked mixture using a potato masher. Add the garlic and salt. Stir to blend.

Return the saucepan to low heat and simmer for about 2 minutes, stirring a few times.

Adjust the salt to taste.

Serve with *Chiles Relleños*.

"Mexican Breakfast"

"Mexican breakfast," as we call it on both sides of the border, refers to very specific dishes such as eggs cooked with corn tortillas, *migas*, or *gorditas*. "Mexican Breakfast" is frequently eaten in small cafés that close in the afternoon, as dinner is most often eaten at home, at least during the week. Going out for "Mexican breakfast" is a family event on weekends. Also available in these spots is an "American breakfast." That refers to typical café combinations eaten in the morning: bacon or ham and eggs with toast.

Frontera Gorditas

Made with dough similar to that for tamales, *gorditas* are so good your knees will buckle when you taste them. Especially if you use lard! Shortening will do, but *gorditas*, meaning "little fat ones," are even better made with lard. They can be eaten plain or split and filled with cheese, *Pollo Guisado* (page 45), *Carne Guisada* (page 134), or *Puerco Guisada* (page 133)—stewed chicken, beef, or pork. Other filling possibilities include refried beans (page 164) or any variation of scrambled eggs. *Gorditas* are the much-beloved breakfast "bread" of South Texas. The Boca Chica HEB Supermarket deli in Brownsville does a huge business every morning with *gorditas* to-go.

Makes 12 gorditas

2 cups *masa harina* (instant corn flour)
1 teaspoon salt
1 teaspoon baking powder
1½ cups unsalted chicken broth
½ cup lard or vegetable shortening
Vegetable oil

Preheat a *comal* or griddle over low heat.

In a large mixing bowl, combine the *masa*, salt, and baking powder, using a whisk to blend well.

In a small saucepan over low heat, combine the broth and lard. Heat to melt the lard. Set aside off the heat to cool to lukewarm before combining with the dry ingredients.

Add the lukewarm liquid to the dry ingredients and knead for about 5 minutes.

Divide the dough into 12 golf ball–size rounds, about 1 ounce each.

Lightly oil the preheated *comal* or griddle.

Press the balls into ½-inch-thick patties or *gorditas*. Grill the *gorditas* over low heat for a total of 10 to 12 minutes, turning as needed to prevent overbrowning. *Gorditas* should cook slowly so the inside isn't too doughy. The outside should have light brown spots.

Serve plain or split with a knife (as you would an English muffin).

Assemble as opposite and serve immediately.

Breakfast *Gorditas* assembly

Makes 12 *gorditas*

12 *Gorditas* (see page 144)

2 cups filling, such as *Pollo Guisado* (page 45), *Carne Guisada* (page 134),
    Puerco Guisada (page 133), refried beans (page 164), *Migas* (page 147), or
    "Mexican Breakfast" Potatoes (page 148)

2 cups shredded *queso fresco* (optional)

Split a *gordita* as you would a pita. For a pocket; do not cut all the way through.

Fill with 2 tablespoons of the desired filling. Top with queso fresco, if desired.

Chilaquiles con Salsa Verde
CRISPY TORTILLA PIECES WITH GREEN SAUCE

This beautiful breakfast side dish, sautéed tortilla pieces in a spicy green sauce, is often eaten with scrambled eggs. Some versions call for scrambling the eggs with the tortillas to make *Migas* (see opposite). That's not the version I grew up eating. Mine is the authentic Rio Grande way. *Salsa Verde* in this recipe is similar to, but not the same as, the *Salsa Verde* (page 38) I use for enchiladas. This recipe is a bit spicier and thicker and uses Mexican oregano (page 98).   **Makes 6 servings**

1½ pounds tomatillos, rinsed after peeling papery outer skin, cut in half

1½ cups chopped yellow onions

1 (3-inch) jalapeño, stem removed and cut in half

1 large tomato, cut into quarters

1 teaspoon dried Mexican oregano

2 garlic cloves

2 teaspoons salt

2 tablespoons plus 2 cups vegetable oil

12 corn tortillas

1 cup shredded *queso fresco*

In a large saucepan over high heat, combine the tomatillos, 1 cup of the onions, the jalapeño, tomato, oregano, and 2½ cups water. Bring to a boil, then reduce the heat, cover, and simmer gently for 20 minutes. Set aside off the heat to cool slightly.

In a blender jar or work bowl of a food processor, process the tomatillo mixture, garlic, and salt on high speed for about 2 minutes, until smooth. Set aside.

In a large saucepan over medium heat, warm the 2 tablespoons oil. Add the remaining ½ cup onions and cook until the onions are translucent and soft but not browned, about 3 minutes. Add the blended tomatillo mixture. Stir to combine. Keep warm.

In a large skillet over medium-high heat, heat the remaining 2 cups oil to 350°F.

While the oil is heating, cut the tortillas into 1-inch squares.

When oil reaches 350°F, carefully slide one third of the tortilla squares in the hot oil and fry for 1 to 2 minutes, until light golden and crispy. Using a slotted spoon, remove the fried tortilla pieces and set aside on paper towels to drain excess oil. Fry the remaining tortillas in two more batches.

Discard the oil and wipe the skillet clean. Return the fried tortilla pieces to the skillet. Pour the sauce over the crispy tortilla pieces to cover.

Sprinkle with the cheese. Serve immediately.

Migas con Huevos a la Mexicana

SCRAMBLED EGGS WITH CRISPY TORTILLAS, ONIONS, AND PEPPERS

Migas is a favorite breakfast dish of scrambled eggs with pieces of corn tortilla. Some folks grew up on *migas* made with crispy tortilla pieces; others with lightly sautéed, instead of crispy, tortilla pieces. I prefer them crispy, but adjust the cooking time as you like. This recipe is "*a la Mexicana*" because it includes chopped tomato, onion, and jalapeño.   *Makes 4 servings*

2 cups plus 1 tablespoon
   vegetable oil
8 corn tortillas
½ cup chopped white onion
1 tablespoon chopped jalapeño
½ cup chopped tomato
4 large eggs, lightly beaten
2 cups shredded Monterey Jack
   cheese (optional)

Preheat the oven to 350°F.

In a large ovenproof skillet over medium-high heat, heat the 2 cups oil to 350°F.

While the oil is heating, cut the tortillas into 1-inch squares.

When the oil is hot, carefully slide half of the tortilla squares into the oil and fry until they are slightly golden and crispy, about 3 to 4 minutes. Using a slotted spoon, remove the fried tortilla pieces and set aside on paper towels to drain excess oil. Repeat with the remaining tortilla squares.

Discard the oil and wipe the skillet clean. Place the skillet over low heat with 1 tablespoon oil. Add the onion and cook until soft but not brown, about 3 minutes. Stir in the jalapeño and cook for 30 seconds. Add the tomato and cook for 1 minute, or just until the tomatoes are heated through.

Place half of the fried tortilla pieces in the pan, stirring to combine with the vegetables.

Pour the beaten eggs over the mixture and cook over low heat until the egg is set, about 2 minutes. Remove from the heat.

Sprinkle the eggs with the remaining tortillas and the cheese, if desired. Place in the oven for 3 to 5 minutes to melt the cheese. Serve immediately.

"Mexican Breakfast" Potatoes

No weekend breakfast at my home and few at my restaurants are complete without this brunch favorite. Whether served alongside eggs or rolled in a flour tortilla as a breakfast taco, a sauté of bacon and potatoes starts the day off right.

Bacon, with onion and garlic, give these potatoes a fabulous flavor. Cayenne is an optional add-on just before serving. Children usually find it too spicy.

Makes 6 servings

2 pounds russet (peeled) or red
    potatoes (unpeeled), cut into
    ½- inch pieces

2 teaspoons salt

8 ounces thick bacon, cut into
    ½-inch pieces

1 cup thinly sliced white onion

3 garlic cloves, minced

⅛ teaspoon cayenne pepper
    (optional)

In a medium saucepan over high heat, combine the potatoes, 1½ quarts water, and 1½ teaspoons of the salt. Bring to a boil, then lower the heat and simmer for 8 minutes. Pour the potatoes into a colander to drain. Run cool water over the potatoes for 1 minute to stop the cooking process. Set aside.

In a large skillet over medium heat, cook the bacon for 5 to 7 minutes, until crispy. Using a slotted spoon, remove the bacon to paper towels to drain. Set aside.

Pour the bacon grease into a heatproof bowl or cup. Return 3 tablespoons bacon grease to the skillet.

Over medium heat, add the onion to the bacon grease and cook for about 2 minutes. Add the garlic, the remaining ½ teaspoon salt, and the cayenne, if desired. Cook until the onion is tender, about 3 minutes.

Add the potatoes and stir gently. If the potatoes are not completely cooked, cook over low heat, stirring occasionally, until the potatoes can be easily pierced with a fork.

Serve immediately.

Huevos Rancheros
EGGS WITH RANCHERA SAUCE

Fried eggs on tortillas with red chile sauce is a legendary breakfast dish of Mexico and South Texas. A great *Salsa Ranchera* (page 31) is what makes *Huevos Rancheros* really special.

The hard part of this is to fry the eggs without breaking the yolks. Ideally, eggs for *Huevos Rancheros* are cooked medium so that the beautiful yellow yolk, when pierced with a fork, blends with the piquant sauce.

I developed this method of preparing eggs sunny side up so I don't have to flip them and risk breaking the yolk. This technique also makes it possible to cook eggs for more than one or two servings. If I'm serving *Huevos Rancheros* for entertaining, I use two or three nonstick pans so I can cook more eggs at once and have them ready at about the same time. Set up an assembly line with 2 eggs broken into each of six bowls. Or just fry eggs in oil or bacon grease.

Some guests prefer this dish without a corn tortilla. The recipe is simplified somewhat if the corn tortilla is omitted, which is frequently done.

Serve with Refried Beans (page 164), bacon, and "Mexican Breakfast" Potatoes (page 148).

Makes 6 servings

Special Equipment

- As many as six small bowls
- Two or three medium nonstick skillets with lids

6 corn tortillas
½ cup (1 stick) unsalted butter, melted
12 large eggs
3 cups *Salsa Ranchera* (page 31), warm

Preheat a *comal* or heavy griddle over low heat.

Brush each tortilla on one side with butter and place buttered side down on the griddle. Brush the top side of the tortilla with butter. Cook the tortilla for about 2 minutes, turn, and cook on the other side for 2 minutes. Repeat until all the tortillas have been griddled. Keep warm.

In a medium nonstick skillet(s) over medium heat, heat 1 tablespoon melted butter (per skillet) until the butter sizzles, about 2 minutes.

Into a small dish (or each of six dishes), break 2 eggs. Remove any pieces of shell.

Carefully pour 2 eggs into each skillet and cover with a tight-fitting lid. Cook over low heat for 2 to 4 minutes, depending on whether you want your eggs very soft or almost hard.

Arrange the griddled tortillas on six dinner plates. Place a pair of cooked eggs on each tortilla. Pour ½ cup *Salsa Ranchera* over the eggs and each tortilla and serve immediately.

CHAPTER 8

TAMALE TUTORIAL

A *tamalada* is a tamale-making party. The Enchilada Queen extends an invitation to all of you. Making tamales is a family-and-friends affair. It takes a lot of hands to cook the fillings, soak the dried corn husks, mix the dough, spread the *masa* and fill it, fold the shucks and wrap the tamales, stack them in the steamer, then steam the tamales. And everyone wants to eat.

First, a little background: Tamales have been around for hundreds of years. The Aztecs made them way before the European invasion. Very practical, tamales are among the first examples of take-away in biodegradable packaging. Aztecs could take them to work or to war and have a handheld meal.

You might think that the filling is the key to a good tamale. If so, you're incorrect. The dough (*masa*) is the star of the show. *Masa* makes a tamale's first impression. The filling is important, but *masa* dough is critical. If the dough is light, fluffy, and flavorful, anything in the middle is okay: pork, chicken, beef, vegetables, wild game, beans, or cheese.

Tamales were the subject of the first cooking classes at my restaurant nine years ago. Right before Christmas, I offered a hands-on class. After the class was publicized in *The Houston Chronicle*, the phone rang off the wall. I had several types of students: women of Latin or Mexican descent; women

who didn't learn how to make tamales from mothers and grandmothers and needed a teacher; sisters and cousins who came together to learn so they could start their own tamale-making traditions.

Now I teach four or five tamale-making classes a year. Hands-on, the classes are a lot of fun, though a bit chaotic. Every student makes six tamales to take home and steam.

Because they are labor intensive, homemade tamales are special-occasion food, particularly associated with the holiday season. Whether homemade or purchased (often from a local tamale maker who produces them by the dozen for sale during the holiday season), freshly steamed tamales are a Christmas Eve tradition. My dad used to say, "On Christmas Day, trash cans all over the valley are full of husks."

One reason to make or buy a bunch of tamales is that they're an easy meal or snack during the busy holidays. Mexican women are ingenious that way. With dozens of tamales in the fridge, the answer to the question, "What's for lunch [or breakfast, or dinner]?" is "Tamales," all the way through New Year's Day. That leaves a little time for relaxation or, more likely, other chores. Steamed tamales can be refrigerated for up to a week and frozen for up to three months after that. To reheat tamales, steam them over water on the stove, heat them in the oven, or microwave them.

My family's tamaladas

An invitation to a *tamalada* at my mother's house when my grandmother, Sarita, directed the tamale-making was prized among our friends and family. When they threw a *tamalada*, multiple generations of our family and friends pitched in. The traditional occasion for a *tamalada* is Christmas Eve. We'd turn on the music and catch up on the latest gossip while spreading *masa* on corn husks, filling, then folding and steaming the tamales. When they were ready, we had to eat in shifts because the family dinner table only sat eight—and our tamale-making team was considerably more numerous. My grandmother, the matriarch of our clan, was in charge of *masa*, directing the mixing and flavoring of the dough. My mother oversaw the preparation of the fillings to make sure the flavors were just right. It took a posse of people to do the assembly. We made thirty or forty dozen tamales to be divided among five or six households. Sometimes even that many tamales didn't go that far, especially when we had tamale-eating contests. My brother, Oscar, always challenged the nieces and nephews!

Special equipment

- Large stockpot, sanitized cooler, or big bucket for soaking corn husks
- Food handlers' gloves
- Several serving spoons, 2-inch-wide wall spacklers, or flat-blade spatulas to spread *masa* onto husks
- Small bowls of water in which to dip *masa* spreaders if *masa* builds up
- 20-quart stockpot with steamer rack *or* a tamale steamer
- Heavy cast-iron *comal* or skillet
- Brick wrapped in foil then secured in a plastic bag with zipper closing, optional
- Small coin

Tamalada timeline

2 to 3 days ahead: Prepare filling(s). Store in the refrigerator. Gently reheat before setting up the assembly line.

Early in the day: Soak husks for wrapping tamales 2 to 3 hours before starting the assembly line. Drain the husks when ready to set up the assembly line and spread out in a flat pan. Trim to uniform size, about 6 inches across and 7 to 8 inches in length.

1 to 3 hours before assembly line setup: Prepare the *masa*.

When ready to fill tamales, set up the assembly line in this order:

1. Husks; 2. *Masa;* 3. Filling; 4. Large flat pan or tray for holding folded tamales; 5. Tamale steamer

Soaked Corn Husks for Tamales

2 (8-ounce) bags dried corn
   husks for tamales
1 gallon warm water

In a large container, place the corn husks in the warm water to soak.

Put a heavy object, such as a cast-iron skillet, *comal*, or wrapped brick, on top of the husks to keep them immersed. Soak for several hours before filling tamales.

Drain the husks when ready to set up the assembly line and spread them out in a flat pan. Trim to uniform size, about 6 inches across and 7 to 8 inches in length.

About corn husks

Used to secure the dough and filling for tamales, dried corn husks must be soaked in water to make them soft and pliable. You need a big, deep container, such as large stockpot, sanitized cooler, or bucket, to hold water and husks. You also need a heavy weight to keep them immersed. I like to use a heavy cast-iron skillet, *comal,* or wrapped brick.

For even cooking, corn husks should be approximately the same size. Dimensions should be about 6 inches across and about 7 to 8 inches in length. If the corn husks are much larger, trim to uniform size after soaking.

You need to soak enough husks to accommodate the filling plus some extras for "mistakes" and to cover the tamales that are being steamed. An extra dozen or so is always a good idea.

About *masa* (dough)

Tamale dough, called *masa*, is traditionally mixed by hand, but you may use a heavy-duty mixer with a dough hook. Fresh lard, available in Hispanic meat markets or grocery stores, should be used for the most flavorful results, but vegetable shortening will work.

After mixing, the dough should feel light and fluffy, not heavy. I add just a touch of baking powder to my *masa* to make it goof proof. Another tamale-making trick is to melt the lard before blending with dry ingredients.

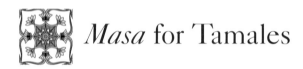

Masa for Tamales

To test for right consistency, pinch off a piece of dough and place it in cold water. It should float. If it doesn't float, mix *masa* for another 5 minutes to more evenly distribute the fat.

Makes enough masa for 10 dozen tamales

5 guajillo chiles, seeds and stems removed

1 (3½-pound) bag (14 cups) *masa harina* (instant corn flour)

6 teaspoons baking powder

4 teaspoons salt

2½ pounds lard or vegetable shortening

3¼ cups pork or chicken stock (reserved from *guisado,* see page 134)

In a medium saucepan over high heat, combine the chiles and 2¼ cups water. Bring to a boil, then reduce the heat and simmer for 15 minutes. Set aside off the heat to cool for about 10 minutes. In a blender, process the chiles and their liquid until smooth. Pour through a fine strainer to remove solids that did not liquefy. Discard the solids. Set aside 1½ cups of the chile sauce to add to the *masa*.

In a large bowl, combine the *masa harina*, baking powder, and salt. Mix well by hand.

In a large saucepan over low heat, combine the lard, stock, the 1½ cups chile sauce, and 3½ cups water. Heat to melt the lard, using a whisk to blend all of the ingredients. Set aside off the heat when lard is melted and well blended. Allow to cool slightly.

To the dry ingredients in the large bowl, add the melted lard mixture, about 3 cups at a time. Mix with a large spoon or use gloved hands to combine. Use a mixer with a dough hook if available.

In the bowl, knead the *masa* until the dough is well blended and light, about 5 minutes. Break off a piece and see if it floats in cold water. If it floats, the dough is ready. If it sinks, knead the dough for an additional 5 minutes to better incorporate the fat.

Cover with plastic wrap and set aside.

Pork or Chicken Tamales

These are basic tamales, filled with pork or chicken.

Makes 10 dozen tamales

11 or 12 dozen soaked corn
   husks (page 154), or as
   needed
1 recipe *masa* for tamales
   (page 155)
6 cups *Puerco* (page 133) or
   Pollo (page 45) *Guisado* for
   tamales

TO ASSEMBLE TAMALES

Arrange an assembly line: soaked corn husks, *masa* dough, and filling.

Place about 2 tablespoons (2 ounces) *masa* dough in the center of the smooth side of a soaked corn husk. The husk will resemble a triangle (wide on one end with long, narrow "tail" at the other end). The outside should be the side with palpable veins or ridges.

Using the back of a tablespoon, wall spackler, or flat-blade spatula, spread *masa* from the wide end, leaving 4 inches uncovered at the narrow "tail" end. There should be about 4 inches from the narrow "tail" end without tamale dough.

Spread *masa* evenly to the side edges of the husk. This will allow the "tail" to fold over the body of the tamale.

Place about 2 tablespoons filling down the center of the *masa*.

Fold the sides of the husk, one at a time, toward the center. They should overlap.

Fold the bottom part of the husk (the narrow "tail" end without *masa*) up. Place the tamale seam down on a platter or flat pan.

Tamales for breakfast

I particularly love tamales for breakfast. To heat them, I place the tamales, husks still on, in a single layer in a heavy skillet over low heat. I put a lid on the skillet and cook for about 30 minutes to toast the husk and crisp the *masa*. Toasted tamales, brown and crispy, are fabulous with coffee.

Repeat until all the *masa* and filling are used. If *masa* is left over, you can use up the *masa* dough by making tamales without filling. Spread, fold, and steam as you would filled tamales. They're just as delicious. Remember, tamales are all about the *masa*!

TO STEAM TAMALES

Ready a 20-quart stockpot with a steamer rack or tamale steamer on the stovetop. Drop a small coin in the bottom of the pot. Add enough water to come up level with the surface of the rack. Note how much water this required.

Invert a shallow heatproof bowl in the center of the rack. Stack the tamales, folded pointed end down, around the bowl like spokes on a wagon wheel. Repeat the layering, staggering tamales so there is some space in between for steam to circulate. Repeat until all the tamales are stacked in the steamer.

Drape flat corn husks over the stack of tamales to trap steam. To further make sure tamales get plenty of hot steam, cover the corn husks with a clean dish towel.

Turn the heat to high to bring the water to a boil. Place the lid on the steamer. When steam starts to rise, lower the heat and cook the tamales over simmering water for about 1 hour 30 minutes. If you hear the coin rattling, that means the water has cooked away. Add more water to the level of steamer rack, based on the initial amount.

After steaming the tamales, turn off the heat but leave the covered pot on the burner for 30 minutes to finish cooking.

To test for doneness, open one tamale. Completely cooked dough should separate easily from the husk. Serve warm.

TO SPREAD MASA

Fill the trimmed husks with about 2 tablespoons of the prepared masa.

Spread the masa over the husks.

Simply Sweet Tamales

Sweet tamales are more for breakfast or snacks, whereas savory tamales, like pork or chicken, are a convenient meal for anytime. Instead of lard, I use butter for sweet tamales. They are also a Christmas Eve tradition with Mexican Hot Chocolate (page 211). Sweet tamales may be filled with stewed apples, coconut and raisins, chopped dates, or any other sweet fruit filling. If you opt not to use a filling, you are making *tamales de elote*, sweet corn tamales. **Makes 40 tamales**

2 (15½-ounce) cans yellow corn

2 cups (4 sticks) unsalted butter

¾ cup unsalted chicken broth

5¼ cups *masa harina* (instant corn flour)

¾ cup sugar

2 tablespoons baking powder

1 teaspoon salt

2 cups sweetened flaked coconut

1¼ cups raisins, soaked in warm water for 10 minutes, then drained

At least 5 dozen soaked corn husks (page 154)

Drain the corn, reserving ½ cup of the corn liquid.

In a blender jar or work bowl of a food processor, process the corn from 1 can for 20 to 30 seconds, until finely chopped. Set aside. Repeat with the remaining corn.

In a medium saucepan over low heat, melt the butter. Add the broth and corn liquid, stirring with a wire whisk to blend. Set aside off the heat.

In a large bowl, combine the *masa harina,* sugar, baking powder, and salt. Mix well by hand.

To the dry ingredients, add the melted butter mixture and chopped corn. In the bowl, knead the *masa* until the dough is well blended and light, about 5 minutes. Break off a piece and see if it floats in cold water. If it floats, the dough is ready. If it sinks, knead the dough for an additional 5 minutes to better incorporate the fat.

TO ASSEMBLE SWEET TAMALES

Arrange an assembly line: soaked corn husks, *masa* dough, and filling.

Place about 2 tablespoons (2 ounces) *masa* dough in the center of a soaked corn husk. The husk will resemble a triangle (wide on one end with long, narrow "tail" at the other end). (See page 157.)

Using the back of a tablespoon, wall spackler, or flat-blade spatula, spread *masa* from the wide end, leaving 4 inches uncovered at the narrow "tail" end. There should be about 4 inches from the narrow "tail" end without tamale dough.

Spread *masa* evenly to the side edges of the husk. This will allow the "tail" to fold over the body of the tamale.

Arrange about 1 tablespoon coconut in a strip down the center of the *masa*. Place about 7 raisins the length of the coconut.

Fold the sides of the husk, one at a time, toward the center. They should overlap.

Fold the bottom part of the husk (the narrow end without *masa*) up. Place the tamale face down on a platter.

Repeat until all the *masa* and filling are used.

TO STEAM SWEET TAMALES

Ready a 20-quart stockpot with a steamer rack on the stovetop or over a standalone heating element. Drop a small coin in the bottom of the pot. Add enough water to come up level with surface of the rack. Note how much water this required.

Invert a shallow heatproof bowl in the center of the rack. Stack the tamales, folded pointed end down, around the bowl like spokes on a wagon wheel. Repeat the layering, staggering the tamales so there is some space in between for steam to circulate. Repeat until all the tamales are stacked in the steamer.

Drape flat corn husks over the stack of tamales to catch steam. To make sure tamales get plenty of hot steam, cover the corn husks with a clean dish towel to trap steam.

Turn the heat to low, place the lid on the steamer, and cook the tamales over simmering water for about 1 hour 30 minutes. If you hear the coin rattling, that means the water has cooked away. Add more water to the level of the steamer rack, based on the initial amount.

After steaming the tamales, turn off the heat but leave the covered pot on the burner for 30 minutes to finish cooking.

To test for doneness, open one tamale. Completely cooked dough should separate easily from the husk. Serve warm.

CHAPTER 9

ENCHILADA QUEEN SIDES

Rice and beans are the ubiquitous sidekicks on a "Mexican food" plate. "Red rice" is the classic version of "Mexican rice." I call it Sarita's Rice, after my Mamá Grande. Made the traditional way, by browning the rice before cooking it in liquid to plump and tenderize, the rice gets its reddish tinge from pureed tomatoes.

Beans are most often pinto, either "refried" or boiled in a savory broth. Black beans have also come into favor in recent years. Although as a *frontera* kid, no one ever served me black beans.

Grilled onions and peppers are another mainstay of Rio Grande cooking. Grilled meats and poultry, including fajitas, are often served on top or alongside thereof. Also roasted corn, *elotes*; I do it the Mexican "street corn" way, spread with a coating of mayonnaise and sprinkled with my delicious seasoning blend.

Rice

"Mexican rice" is distinguished by the red color of the grains and the technique of toasting or sautéing in oil before boiling. This technique requires long-grain white rice for a good result. If I go into a "Mexican restaurant" and that dish is made with parboiled rice, I know they don't know what they're doing. Parboiled rice puffs like popcorn instead of browning; then it won't absorb the liquid that plumps and tenderizes it. It simply doesn't work for these traditional recipes.

Sarita's Rice

Sarita's Rice is a third-generation recipe that I learned from my mother, who learned it from her mother. My grandmother, Sarita, loved rice, so there was always a pot of it on her stove. This is the first recipe I prepared in my mom's kitchen, at age eleven, to surprise my parents when they returned home from work. I had watched Mom prepare this recipe time and time again. I am not exactly sure how close I got to her recipe, but I stepped out with a fair level of confidence and went for it. They were so surprised and happy to come home to find dinner ready. And the house smelled great. Today my granddaughter, Beth, loves this rice recipe and won't eat anyone's rice but mine. I hope it will one day be a fourth-generation rice recipe. **Makes 6 servings**

½ cup tomato cut into wedges
½ cup chopped white onion
2¼ cups chicken stock (page 18)
2 tablespoons vegetable oil
1 cup long-grain white rice
3 tablespoons tomato sauce
2 teaspoons Tex-Mex Holy
    Trinity (page 20)
1 teaspoon salt

In a blender jar or work bowl of a food processor, process the tomato, onion, and ¼ cup of the broth for 30 seconds to 1 minute, until smooth. Set aside.

In a large skillet over medium heat, heat oil until it shimmers. Add the rice and cook, stirring frequently, for 3 to 5 minutes, until the rice turns a golden brown.

Carefully stir in the blended tomato mixture, the remaining 2 cups broth, the tomato sauce, Holy Trinity, and salt.

Over high heat, bring to a boil, then reduce the heat, cover, and simmer for 15 minutes. Set aside off the heat, covered, for 5 minutes. Fluff the rice with a fork and serve hot.

Arroz Verde

GREEN RICE

Though delicious, *Arroz Verde* isn't traditional to my home region. This is my contribution to the Rio Grande cuisine repertoire, a recipe I developed to serve with fish dishes. Cilantro gives it color and punch. Toasted corn adds another touch of color and crunch.

Makes 6 servings

½ cup coarsely chopped yellow onion

1 garlic clove

½ cup loosely packed fresh cilantro leaves

2⅓ cups chicken stock (page 18), heated to almost boiling

1 teaspoon vegetable oil

1 tablespoon unsalted butter

1 cup long-grain white rice

2 teaspoons chicken base or Knorr chicken bouillon

¼ teaspoon ground white pepper

½ teaspoon salt

½ cup fresh or frozen corn, toasted (see below)

½ cup shredded Monterey Jack cheese

In a blender jar or work bowl of a food processor, process the onion, garlic, cilantro, and ½ cup of the broth. Process for about 30 seconds, until smooth. Set aside.

In a large skillet over low heat, combine the oil and butter. When bubbly, stir in the rice and cook, stirring frequently, for 3 to 5 minutes, until the rice is lightly browned.

Carefully add the remaining hot broth, the chicken base, white pepper, and salt, stirring to combine. Reduce the heat, cover, and simmer for 15 minutes. Set aside off the heat, covered, for 5 minutes. Fluff with a fork.

Gently stir in the corn and cheese and serve.

To pan-toast corn

Preheat a small skillet over medium heat. Add 1 tablespoon butter. When the butter is bubbly, add the corn and cook, stirring frequently, until toasted, medium brown in color, 3 to 5 minutes.

Beans

Beans, whether refried, *charros*, or simply seasoned and cooked in a clay pot and known as *frijoles de olla*, are a daily staple in Rio Grande homes. Pintos are the traditional beans of choice, served boiled and mashed. "Refried" or mashed pinto beans, also called *refritos*, are what is usually found in homes and in restaurants. Even without meat or poultry, beans combined with rice or corn tortillas make a complete protein. Beans are the reason many cultures have survived through hard times.

These recipes make large amounts. Beans freeze and reheat beautifully. So keep the leftovers until your next "Mexican food" cooking binge.

The Enchilada Queen's Fabulous Refried Beans

My grandmother prepared beans almost daily, so they were always super fresh. I recall Mom made certain her beans were well seasoned, so when I developed my recipe, I replicated her flavors. A lot of folks think lard is a requirement for flavorful, creamy refried beans. Not so. My mother did not use lard in her beans, so neither have I, at home or in my restaurants.

Beans are so important to Rio Grande cuisine. This very flavorful version of beans is a culinary manifestation of my border heritage.

Getting the consistency you like is one of the keys to great refried beans. Traditionally, beans are made the old-fashioned way with a potato masher and elbow grease. A blender, food processor, or immersion blender may also be used.

Makes 12 servings

1⅓ cups dry pinto beans
1½ cups chopped white onions
3 garlic cloves, minced
2 small dried *chiles pequin*,
   finely chopped; or
     ¼ teaspoon cayenne pepper
2 teaspoons salt
½ cup vegetable oil
⅛ teaspoon cayenne pepper
   (optional)

Pick through the beans to remove any impurities or shriveled beans. Place in a large bowl with enough water to cover. Remove any beans that float. Pour the beans and water into a colander to drain. Rinse the beans thoroughly with cold water.

In a large saucepan, Dutch oven, or stockpot over high heat, combine 6 cups water, the rinsed beans, 1 cup of the onions, 2 of the minced garlic cloves, the dried chiles, and salt. Bring to a boil, then reduce the heat, cover, and simmer for about 1 hour 30 minutes, or until the beans are soft, with no chalkiness to the bite.

Using an immersion blender or potato masher, process or mash the beans until they are of desired consistency, smooth to lumpy, however you prefer.

In a large skillet over medium-high heat, heat the oil until it shimmers. Add the remaining ½ cup onions and cook for about 5 minutes, stirring frequently, until soft but not brown. Add the remaining garlic and cook for 2 minutes. The onions will be slightly golden.

Stir the mashed beans into the onions and lower the heat. Simmer for another 10 minutes, stirring occasionally. Add additional cayenne pepper as desired. Serve hot.

Enchilada Queen Quick Refried Beans

It's okay to use canned beans to make refried beans. You're just shortcutting the process of cooking dried beans. Yes, the flavor profile may not be quite as vibrant if you don't cook and season them yourself, but there's still plenty of flavor in less than half the time. Not a bad trade-off.

This shortcut recipe works with pinto or black beans. You won't sacrifice too much flavor for convenience gained. These are quick and easy and taste great. **Makes 6 servings**

2 (14½-ounce) cans pinto or black beans, undrained
¼ cup vegetable oil
1 cup chopped yellow onion
3 garlic cloves, minced
¼ teaspoon cayenne pepper
¼ teaspoon salt, or more to taste
⅛ teaspoon freshly ground black pepper

In a blender jar or work bowl of a food processor, process 1 can of beans on low speed for about 1 minute. Repeat with the remaining beans. Set aside.

In a large saucepan over medium heat, heat the oil until it shimmers. Add the onion and garlic and cook for 4 to 5 minutes, until golden brown, stirring constantly.

Add the cayenne pepper and cook for another 1 minute.

Add the beans, salt, and black pepper. Lower the heat and gently cook for 3 to 4 minutes, stirring frequently.

Adjust the seasoning with salt.

Set aside off the heat to cool for about 5 minutes, then serve.

Sylvia's *Charro* Beans

This is another version of pinto beans, this time served whole, unmashed. In South Texas, these beans are very popular with grilled plates, such as fajitas. These are called *charro*, i.e. cowboy-style, beans.

Makes 12 servings

2 cups dry pinto beans

2 teaspoons salt

6 ounces bacon, cut into 1-inch strips

1 cup chopped white onion

½ cup chopped green bell pepper

3 garlic cloves, minced

1 cup chopped tomato

1 cup chopped fresh cilantro

Pick through the beans to remove any impurities or shriveled beans. Place in a large bowl with enough water to cover. Remove any beans that float. Pour the beans and water into a colander to drain. Rinse thoroughly with cold water.

In a large saucepan or stockpot over high heat, combine the rinsed beans, 10 cups water, and the salt. Bring to a boil, then reduce the heat, cover, and simmer for 1 hour. Set aside off the heat.

In a medium skillet over medium heat, cook the bacon until crispy. Add the onion, bell pepper, and garlic. Cook, stirring occasionally, for 3 to 4 minutes, until the onion is soft and brown at the edges.

To the beans, add the bacon and onion mixture, the tomato, and cilantro. Place over high heat. Bring to a boil, then reduce the heat and simmer for about 10 minutes. Beans should be soft, with no chalkiness to the bite. If the beans are still a little firm, cook for an additional 5 minutes, or until tender. Do not overcook the beans or they will soften and turn to mush instead of remaining whole.

Serve hot.

To grind dried chiles

Remove the stems (and seeds when required) from peppers. Using a mini-chopper, *molcajete*, or mortar and pestle, combine the chiles with 1 tablespoon water. Process until smooth.

Enchilada Queen *Frijoles Negros*
BLACK BEANS

Black beans are not at all South Texas, but after repeated customer requests, I developed a recipe for *frijoles negros*. Very popular, these beans are slightly spicy. If you prefer black beans, substitute them whenever pinto beans are called for. Notice this recipe calls for epazote, an herb that is popular in Mexican cooking, both for its flavor and its reputation as an antidote to "gassy" beans. If you can't find epazote, don't sweat it. Just make the recipe without. There's really no flavor substitute. Beano or a similar product can lessen the uncomfortable side effect of eating beans.

Makes 12 servings

2 cups dry black beans

1½ cups chopped white onions

3 garlic cloves, peeled and finely chopped

2½ teaspoons salt

1 fresh epazote sprig (optional)

¼ cup vegetable oil

3 (3-inch long) *chiles de árbol*, ground (see page 166)

Pick through the beans to remove any impurities or shriveled beans. Place in a large bowl with enough water to cover. Remove any beans that float. Pour the beans and water into a colander to drain. Rinse thoroughly with cold water.

In a large saucepan or medium stockpot over high heat, combine the beans, 8 cups water, 1 cup of the onions, the garlic, 2 teaspoons of the salt, and the epazote, if using. Bring to a boil, then reduce the heat, cover, and simmer for 1 hour 45 minutes. Beans should be soft, with no chalkiness to the bite. If the beans are still a little firm, cook for an additional 5 minutes, or until tender.

In a small skillet over medium heat, combine the oil and the remaining ½ cup onions. Cook until the onions are lightly browned, about 5 minutes.

To the beans, add the browned onions, ground dried chiles, and the remaining ½ teaspoon salt; simmer for 5 minutes.

Remove the epazote sprig and discard it. Serve the beans hot.

For refried black beans: Using an immersion blender or potato masher, process or mash the cooked black beans until they are of the desired consistency, smooth to lumpy, however you prefer.

More Sides

 Frontera Grilled Onions and Peppers

Grilled onions and peppers are traditional with beef or chicken fajitas. These veggies also may be cooked in a skillet on the stove. Besides fajitas, this side goes great with any grilled beef or chicken, Grilled Quail (page 119), or Rockport Shrimp (page 114).   **Makes 6 servings**

2 tablespoons vegetable oil

4 garlic cloves, minced

4 cups thinly sliced onions

2 cups thinly sliced bell pepper

1½ teaspoons Enchilada Queen
   Seasoning Blend (page 22)

In a large skillet over medium heat, heat the oil until it shimmers. Add the garlic and cook for about 2 minutes.

Add the onions, bell peppers, and Seasoning Blend; cook, stirring frequently, for 8 to 10 minutes, until the onion and peppers are tender and brown at the edges.

Cover and set aside off the heat for 5 minutes, then serve.

To roast garlic

Preheat small heavy skillet over high heat. Add the garlic and cook, turning frequently, until brown, about 5 minutes. Turn out of the skillet and let cool.

Poblano Grits

A plate of Grilled Quail (page 119) isn't complete without a side of Poblano Grits. This creamy, sort of southern, sort of Texas dish is rich and a great pairing with the smoky flavor of meat or poultry off the grill.

Makes 8 servings

3½ cups chicken stock (page 18)

½ cup (1 stick) unsalted butter

1 teaspoon onion powder

2 teaspoons freshly ground black pepper

1 teaspoon salt

1 cup quick-cooking (5-minute) white grits

3 garlic cloves, roasted (see page 168)

3 medium poblano peppers, roasted (see below) and chopped

1 to 2 (2-inch) jalapeños, cut in half, seeds removed if desired

2 large eggs, lightly beaten

3 cups shredded cheddar cheese

1 cup chopped fresh cilantro

In a large saucepan over high heat, combine the broth, butter, onion powder, black pepper, salt, and grits. Bring to a boil, then reduce the heat and simmer, stirring every 2 minutes, for 7 minutes, or until liquid is absorbed. Set aside off the heat for 10 minutes.

Preheat the oven to 350°F. Spray eight ½-cup ramekins or a 9 × 5 × 2¾-inch loaf pan with cooking spray.

In a blender jar or work bowl of a food processor, combine the roasted garlic, poblano peppers, and jalapeños with the eggs. Process just until smooth and slightly thickened. Set aside.

In a large bowl, combine the grits, egg mixture, 2 cups of the cheese, and cilantro. Mix with a rubber spatula until well blended.

Spoon the grits into the prepared ramekins or baking dish. Bake for 15 to 20 minutes, until bubbly at the edges.

Sprinkle the remaining 1 cup cheese over the top. Serve hot.

To roast poblano peppers

Preheat the broiler or a heavy skillet on the stovetop. Place the peppers on a broiler pan or in the hot skillet. Cook until most of the skin blisters and chars. Place in a plastic bag and let cool enough to handle. Holding the stem or stem end, peel off the skin. Remove the stem. Cut open the pepper and scrape out the seeds.

Rajas Poblanas
ROASTED POBLANOS IN CREMA

If Poblano Grits is a hybrid dish, *Rajas Poblanos* is pure Mexico. I sometimes have to assure my customers that it is very mild. The *crema*, a cross between crème fraîche and Greek yogurt, tames the poblano heat.

Makes 6 servings

5 (5-inch) poblano peppers,
   roasted (see page 169)
2 tablespoons unsalted butter
3 garlic cloves, minced
1 yellow onion, sliced
1¼ cups *crema* or crème fraîche
¼ teaspoon salt

Cut the roasted peppers into ½-inch squares.

In a medium skillet over medium heat, melt the butter until bubbly. Add the garlic and cook, stirring frequently, for about 2 minutes. Add the onion and continue to cook until the onion is light golden around the edges, 3 to 5 minutes.

Add the peppers, *crema*, and salt; warm over low heat for about 2 minutes. Do not boil. Set aside off the heat for at least 5 minutes to develop the flavors, then serve.

Nopales Frescos
FRESH CHOPPED CACTUS LEAVES SALAD

Nopales are the tender, delicious inside of the pads (leaves) of a prickly pear cactus. Peel away the prickly outer cover and inside is a beautiful green vegetable with a taste reminiscent of green beans. Fresh *nopales* are available in Hispanic markets or through sources listed in the Resource List (page 213).

Filling a fresh avocado with marinated *Nopales Frescos* salad is a beautiful and refreshing dish.

Makes 6 servings

1 large yellow onion, peeled and cut into 4 pieces

2 garlic cloves, lightly crushed

2 teaspoons salt

1½ pounds *nopales*, chopped and rinsed, about 6 cups

1¼ cups lightly packed fresh cilantro leaves

2 cups grape tomatoes, sliced in half, rinsed, and drained

1¼ cups chopped red onions (same size pieces as the *nopales*)

1 teaspoon garlic powder

1 tablespoon olive oil

Juice of ½ lime, plus 2 limes cut into 6 wedges each

3 large avocados (see Enchilada Queen Avocado Wisdom, page 90), unpeeled, cut in half, pits removed

2 limes, each cut into 6 wedges

In a 1-quart saucepan, combine 2½ cups water, the yellow onion, garlic cloves, and 1 teaspoon salt. Bring to a boil, then reduce the heat and simmer for 10 minutes.

Add the *nopales* and simmer for *only* 2 minutes.

Pour into a colander to drain. Rinse with cold water and drain well. Remove and discard the onion and garlic cloves.

In a medium bowl, combine the *nopales*, cilantro, tomatoes, and red onions, tossing well to evenly distribute the ingredients. Add the garlic powder, oil, and lime juice. Toss again to coat all ingredients. Refrigerate for 1 hour.

While the salad is chilling, scoop the avocado flesh out of the skins. Reserve the skins. Place the scooped-out avocado in a bowl and coarsely mash. Spoon the mashed avocado into the reserved avocado skins. Form a hollow spot in the center.

Spoon the *nopales* salad into the avocado halves. Serve each with 2 slices of lime.

Elotes
ROASTED CORN

When it comes to corn, what's old is new again. Mexicans have been roasting corn for centuries. In recent years, this tradition has been rediscovered as part of the Mexico street food movement. In Mexico, roasted corn usually has a few charred spots, which enhance the natural sweetness.

Served with a light schmear of mayonnaise and a sprinkle of the Enchilada Queen Grilled Vegetable Seasoning Blend, this roasted corn raises the ante. I suggest using mesquite wood or flavoring chips on the grill to add still another flavor dimension.

The seasoning blend also works well as a finishing seasoning on other grilled vegetables such as yellow or green squash, cauliflower "steaks," butternut squash, and sweet potato, or fruit such as pineapple.

If you don't want to heat up the grill, you may cook the corn, husks on, in the microwave.

Makes 6 servings

- Charcoal or gas grill
- Heatproof gloves
- Long grill tongs

6 ears corn on the cob, with
    husks on
4 tablespoons unsalted butter,
    melted
Enchilada Queen Grilled
    Vegetable Seasoning Blend
    (page 23)
½ cup mayonnaise blended
    with ⅛ teaspoon cayenne or
    to taste
Lime wedges

Pull back the corn husks, being careful not to tear them from the cob. Remove the corn silks and replace the husks over and around the corn.

Place the corn, still in its husks, in a very clean stoppered sink or plastic tub, add enough water to cover, and let soak for at 30 minutes.

Light a wood or hardwood charcoal fire at least 30 minutes before you are ready to cook. Coals are ready when covered with a light coating of gray ash. Or preheat a gas grill to medium-high for 30 minutes.

Roast the corn for 15 to 20 minutes, turning about every 5 minutes. Wearing heavy heatproof gloves, pull back the husks. Return the corn to the grill for about 5 minutes, until a few of the kernels are browned or lightly charred.

If the husks get too dry and the corn begins to burn, wrap the corn in foil and continue to roast until the corn is cooked.

When the corn is tender and lightly charred in a few spots, remove from the fire. Tear away the husks and brush the corn with melted butter.

Sprinkle lightly with the seasoning blend.

Serve with cayenne-laced mayonnaise, additional seasoning blend, and lime wedges.

To microwave corn in the husks

Place 3 ears of corn, husks on, in a microwave oven. Cook on high power for 3 to 4 minutes. Set aside, husks on. Repeat with the remaining 3 pieces of corn. When all the ears have been cooked, tear away the husks and prepare as above with butter, seasoning blend, cayenne-laced mayonnaise, and lime wedges.

Esquites
PAN-FRIED CORN WITH CILANTRO

This dish is traditionally made with fresh epazote. Since epazote may be difficult to find outside Hispanic communities, cilantro may be substituted. The flavor of cilantro is wonderful: not the same as epazote, but very good.

Makes 8 servings

¼ cup unsalted butter

1½ cups chopped yellow onions

8 cups frozen sweet corn kernels

1 tablespoon minced seeded jalapeño

1 cup finely chopped fresh cilantro leaves, or ½ cup chopped fresh epazote leaves

1 teaspoon garlic powder

¾ teaspoon salt

In a medium skillet over medium heat, melt the butter.

Add the onions and cook for 3 to 4 minutes, until the onion is soft and translucent.

Stir in the corn, jalapeño, cilantro or epazote, garlic powder, and salt.

Reduce the heat to low and cook for about 10 minutes, then serve.

Ruby Red Grapefruit and Avocado Salad

Healthful, beautiful, and delicious ruby red grapefruit are a signature crop of the Lower Rio Grande Valley. Millions are shipped all over the United States and internationally as holiday gifts (see Resource List, page 213). This salad and the dressing both use fresh mint cut into thin strips known as chiffonade (see below).

Makes 6 servings

2 large ruby red grapefruit

3 large avocados (see Enchilada Queen Avocado Wisdom, page 90), coarsely chopped, about 3 cups

1 cup pecan halves, not toasted

¾ cup chilled Grapefruit Vinaigrette (page 178), or as needed

¾ cup thinly sliced fresh mint leaf or chiffonade (see below)

1 cup crumbled *queso fresco* (optional)

Peel the grapefruit by removing the outer skin. Carefully separate the sections. Remove the membrane from each section and cut the sections into cubes. Place the chopped grapefruit in a medium salad bowl; you should have about 3 cups.

Add the avocado pieces to the salad bowl and toss gently with the grapefruit pieces.

Add the pecans and Grapefruit Vinaigrette; toss gently.

Garnish with mint and crumbled cheese, if desired.

To chiffonade

Stack as many as 10 leaves of mint, basil, spinach, or any other flat leaf. Roll lengthwise into a tight cigar shape. Using a sharp knife, cut across the rolled leaves. The closer together the slices, the finer the chiffonade. Fluff the chiffonade with your fingers to separate the strips before measuring or using as a garnish.

Grapefruit Vinaigrette

This delicious dressing would also complement a spinach (another example of Lower Rio Grande Valley produce) salad with grapefruit and pecans from the official State Tree of Texas.

Makes 2 cups

½ teaspoon caraway seeds

½ cup olive oil

¼ cup balsamic vinegar

¼ cup fresh orange juice

4 teaspoons honey

1 tablespoon minced red onion

1 garlic clove, smashed

5 fresh mint leaves, cut into chiffonade (see page 177)

⅛ teaspoon salt

⅛ teaspoon freshly ground black pepper

In a small skillet over medium heat, toast the caraway seeds for about 3 minutes, until fragrant and very lightly browned. Be careful not to overcook.

In a *molcajete*, mortar and pestle, or spice or coffee grinder, coarsely process the caraway seeds. Do not overprocess to a fine powder.

In a container with a tight-fitting lid, combine the caraway, oil, vinegar, orange juice, honey, onion, garlic, mint, salt, and pepper. Cover and shake well. Refrigerate 1 hour or so for the flavors to blend.

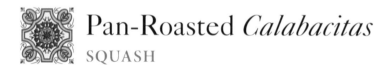

Pan-Roasted *Calabacitas*
SQUASH

Use zucchini for this pretty vegetable dish if lighter green *calabacitas* aren't available. With either variety of squash, this Tex-Mex stir-fry will pretty up a plate. *Makes 8 servings*

3 garlic cloves, minced

¾ teaspoon whole black peppercorns

2 tablespoons unsalted butter

1 cup chopped white onion

6 small *calabacitas* (about 1½ pounds), unpeeled and cut into ½-inch cubes

2 cups frozen sweet corn kernels

1 cup chopped tomato

1 teaspoon minced seeded jalapeño

½ teaspoon dried thyme

½ teaspoon salt

¼ cup chicken stock (page 18) or vegetable broth

In a mortar and pestle, *molcajete*, or spice or coffee grinder, combine the garlic, black peppercorns, and 1 tablespoon water. Process to make a smooth paste. Set aside.

In a large skillet over medium heat, melt the butter. Add the onion and cook for 3 to 4 minutes, until the onion soft and transluscent.

Add the *calabacitas*, corn, tomato, jalapeño, garlic and pepper seasoning paste, thyme, salt, and broth to the skillet.

Cook over medium heat for about 7 minutes, until the *calabacitas* are tender.

Serve with a slotted spoon or drain the excess broth, using the back of a spoon to pour the liquid from the pan.

CHAPTER 10

ENCHILADA QUEEN SWEET ENDINGS

Mexican desserts are not as sweet as those that typical *norteamericanos* love. Most desserts at Sylvia's Enchilada Kitchen are adaptations: Mexican flavors and techniques developed to please my customers. Sweet but not *too* sweet.

Chocolate *Tres Leches* Cake (page 187) is an all-time customer favorite. It was created as a happy homage to Valentine's Day. This chapter also includes classic homestyle baked goods like Pumpkin Empanadas (page 197) and *polvorones*, Mexican cinnamon cookies (page 195). These are wonderful with Mexican Vanilla Ice Cream (page 189).

Let's start with a traditional crowd-pleaser: flan.

About Mexican vanilla

Mexican vanilla is prized for its depth of flavor and intensity. Sadly, some producers tarnished the country's reputation for vanilla by making a cheaper, synthetic product with coumarin, banned in the United States. When buying Mexican vanilla, make sure the label is printed in English and the list of ingredients includes vanilla beans. If the price is too good to be true, the product in your hand probably is not real vanilla. Also real vanilla extract is amber in color, never clear. Always use pure vanilla extract, not imitation or synthetic vanilla, no matter where it's from.

Enchilada Queen Classic Flan

My flan has received hundreds of compliments from self-proclaimed connoisseurs. This version is smooth as white satin with three kinds of milk: sweetened condensed, evaporated, and whole. We sell a lot of these desserts for take-away and as individual servings.

If you can find real Mexican vanilla, use it in this dish for the deepest, most aromatic flavor.

To make this, you'll need six ½-cup glass custard cups and a rectangular baking pan large enough to hold the cups in a single layer. This is called a water bath. Or a round 8-inch baking dish and another pan large enough to hold the baking dish. **Makes 6 servings**

Special Equipment

- **Baking dish for flan or six ½-cup glass custard cups**
- **Larger dish for water bath**

1 cup sugar

1 (14-ounce) can sweetened condensed milk

1 (12-ounce) can evaporated milk

⅔ cup whole milk

3 large eggs, lightly beaten

1¾ teaspoons vanilla extract (Mexican vanilla preferred, see page 180)

In a medium saucepan over high heat, combine the sugar and ¼ cup water. Cook, stirring continuously, until the mixture turns deep golden brown, caramel-colored. Set aside off the heat to cool for about 15 minutes. Pour the caramelized sugar into each custard cup to a depth of about ¼ inch, or pour all the caramelized sugar into the bottom of a round baking dish.

Place the cups or baking dish in a rectangular pan, about 1 inch apart. Carefully add enough hot tap water to the pan to come halfway up the sides of the cups. Set aside.

Position a rack in the middle of the oven and preheat the oven to 350°F.

In a large mixing bowl, combine the sweetened condensed milk, evaporated milk, whole milk, eggs, and vanilla. Using a whisk or electric mixer on low speed, blend to combine well.

Carefully fill each custard cup or round baking pan nearly to the top.

Carefully, so as not to slosh water into the custard cups, place the baking pan with the water in the oven. Bake at 350°F for 1 hour 30 minutes or until a knife inserted in the middle of a flan comes out clean. Remove from the oven and set aside to cool for at least 1 hour.

Lift the custard cups or baking dish from the water bath. Dry the sides and cover each cup tightly with plastic wrap and place in the refrigerator to chill for at least 3 hours. *(continued)*

Enchilada Queen Classic Flan (continued)

To serve, loosen the flan from each cup by running a butter knife around the sides. Place a dessert plate on top of the dish. Carefully, but quickly, invert the dish so that flan slides out and caramelized sugar flows nicely around the flan and onto the plate for a mouthwatering presentation. Serve.

Cinnamon Sugar

In a small bowl, blend ½ cup sugar and 1 tablespoon ground cinnamon.

Mexican Cinnamon Sugar

In small bowl, blend ½ cup sugar with 1 tablespoon freshly ground Mexican cinnamon.

About Mexican cinnamon

Mexican cinnamon, or *canela*, is Ceylon or "real" cinnamon and is different from typical ground cinnamon found in most supermarkets. Typical grocery-store cinnamon is cassia, or Saigon cinnamon. Mexican cinnamon is softer, more like vanilla, while cassia is bolder and spicier, the flavor most North Americans are used to. To use Mexican cinnamon, you usually have to grind it yourself: Place Mexican cinnamon sticks between two sheets of plastic wrap. Using a small hammer or mallet, crack the sticks into small pieces before placing in a spice grinder or blender. Process until finely ground. Pass through a fine sieve, such as a tea strainer, to remove larger pieces.

Classic *Tres Leches* Cake

This is a classic dessert from the Latin American dessert repertoire, sponge cake drenched in three kinds of milk—*tres leches*. This dessert was "discovered" by foodies in the 1990s, as I recall. When I started getting requests, I began experimenting. It took months to perfect this recipe.

Makes 12 servings

Cake Batter

10 large eggs
1¾ cups plus 2 tablespoons granulated sugar
1 pound (4 sticks) unsalted butter, softened at room temperature
3¼ cups all-purpose flour
2 tablespoons baking powder

Three Milks or Tres Leches

1 cup whole milk
½ cup sweetened condensed milk
¾ cup evaporated milk
1 teaspoon vanilla extract (Mexican vanilla preferred, see page 180)

Whipped Cream Frosting

8 ounces cream cheese, softened at room temperature
⅓ cup sugar
1 teaspoon vanilla extract (Mexican vanilla preferred, see page 180)
2 cups heavy whipping cream
⅛ teaspoon salt

Place a baking rack in the middle of the oven. Preheat the oven to 350°F. Grease and flour a 9 × 13-inch baking pan.

Make the cake batter: In a large mixing bowl, combine the eggs and beat on high speed with an electric mixer until the eggs are fluffy and light yellow in color.

Add the sugar in four equal parts, mixing on medium speed after each addition.

Add the softened butter in four equal parts, mixing on medium speed after each addition.

Add the flour in four equal parts, mixing on medium speed after each addition.

Add the baking powder, mixing on medium speed until the batter is well blended.

Pour the batter into the prepared baking pan. Bake on the middle rack for 45 to 50 minutes, until a toothpick inserted in the center comes out clean.

Place the cake on a rack to cool for 1 hour. Run a knife around the edges of cake to loosen. Turn the cake out onto a flat sheet pan. Cover tightly with plastic wrap and refrigerate overnight.

Make the three milks: In a large measuring bowl with a handle and spout, combine the whole milk, sweetened condensed milk, evaporated milk, and vanilla. Using an electric mixer on medium speed, blend well.

Using a wooden skewer, poke holes all the way through the cake about ½ inch apart. Slowly pour the three milks over the cake so it soaks in evenly.

Make the whipped cream frosting: Place a medium mixing bowl and beaters or a whisk in the freezer for 30 minutes.

In the chilled bowl, combine the cream cheese and sugar. Using an electric mixer, mix on medium speed until smooth and well blended, about 2 minutes. Add the vanilla and mix for another 30 seconds.

With the mixer on high speed, gradually add the whipping cream. Add the salt. Continue beating until the frosting is stiff enough to form peaks, 3 to 4 minutes longer.

Spread the frosting over the top and sides of the cake. Refrigerate for several hours before serving. Store any leftovers in the refrigerator.

Enchilada Queen Chocolate *Tres Leches* Cake

This recipe came to me as "divine inspiration" just before Valentine's Day 2006. I wanted a new chocolate dessert for my menu but really hadn't had the time or flash of creativity to make it happen. About a week before that mega dining-out holiday, a light flashed. I headed into the kitchen and went on a cake-baking binge. By Valentine's Day, I was ready to roll out Chocolate *Tres Leches* Cake as a holiday special. Customers loved it. Critics and food writers couldn't print enough about it. I had hit the recipe bull's-eye with this one. This cake has won numerous "best of's" in various publications and was featured in *Texas Monthly* magazine. It continues to bring joy to chocolate lovers.

It calls for Abuelita cinnamon-flavored chocolate tablets, traditionally used for Mexican Hot Chocolate (page 211). This product is widely available in Hispanic supermarkets. If Abuelita or Ibarra brands aren't available, substitute top-quality semisweet chocolate, such as Ghirardelli Semi-Sweet Baking Bar, Callebaut semisweet chocolate block, or Baker's Semi-Sweet Baking Chocolate Bar.

Makes 12 servings

Cake Batter

1¼ cups all-purpose flour

¼ cup Hershey's Special Dark cocoa powder

½ teaspoon baking soda

¼ teaspoon salt

1 teaspoon ground cinnamon

¾ cup (1½ sticks) unsalted butter, softened at room temperature

8 ounces semisweet chocolate, coarsely chopped

2 tablets Abuelita Mexican Hot Chocolate, or 2 ounces semisweet chocolate

4 large eggs

1½ cups sugar

1 teaspoon vanilla extract (Mexican vanilla preferred, see page 180)

1 cup buttermilk, at room temperature

(continued)

Place a baking rack in the middle of the oven. Preheat the oven to 350°F. Grease and flour a 9 × 13-inch baking pan.

Make the cake batter: In a medium bowl, combine the flour, cocoa powder, baking soda, salt, and cinnamon. Using a large wooden spoon, stir to combine. Sift the dry ingredients into another bowl and set aside.

In a small metal bowl, combine the butter and semisweet and Mexican chocolates. Place the bowl over a saucepan with ½ inch of simmering water. Or use a double boiler. The bottom of the bowl should be in the water but not touch the bottom of the saucepan. Stir until the mixture is smooth. Set aside off the heat to cool to room temperature.

In a clean medium bowl, combine the eggs, sugar, and vanilla. Using an electric mixer on medium speed, blend well. Add the buttermilk and mix on medium speed until smooth.

Using a whisk, gradually add the chocolate to the egg mixture, mixing until smooth. *continued)*

Enchilada Queen's Chocolate *Tres Leches* Cake *(continued)*

Three Milks Chocolate

1 cup whole milk

1 cup evaporated milk

½ cup sweetened condensed
   milk

¼ cup Hershey's Chocolate
   Syrup

½ teaspoon ground cinnamon

Chocolate Whipped Cream
Frosting

8 ounces cream cheese,
   softened at room
   temperature

½ cup sugar

1 teaspoon vanilla extract
   (Mexican vanilla preferred,
   see page 180)

1 teaspoon ground cinnamon

2 cups heavy whipping cream

3 to 5 tablespoons Hershey's
   Special Dark cocoa powder

⅛ teaspoon salt

With the electric mixer on low speed, gradually add the dry ingredients in three parts, mixing well after each addition. Mix until smooth.

Pour the batter into the prepared pan. Bake for 35 minutes, turning the pan halfway through baking to make sure the cake bakes evenly. Check for doneness by inserting a toothpick in the center of the cake. If it comes out clean, place the cake on a cooling rack. If the toothpick comes out moist with batter, bake the cake for another 5 minutes.

Place the cake on a rack to cool for 1 hour. Run a knife around the edges of the cake to loosen. Turn the cake out onto a flat sheet pan. Peel away the parchment paper. Cover with plastic wrap and refrigerate for 5 to 6 hours, until the cake is well chilled.

Make the three milks chocolate: In a large measuring bowl with a handle and spout, combine the whole milk, evaporated milk, sweetened condensed milk, chocolate syrup, and cinnamon. Using an electric mixer on medium speed, blend well.

Using a wooden skewer, poke holes all the way through the cake about ½ inch apart. Slowly pour the three milks chocolate over the cake so it soaks in evenly.

Make the chocolate whipped cream frosting: Place a medium mixing bowl and beaters or whisk in the freezer for 30 minutes.

In the chilled bowl, combine the cream cheese and sugar. Using an electric mixer on medium speed, mix until smooth and well blended, about 2 minutes. Add the vanilla and cinnamon; mix for another 30 seconds.

With the mixer on high speed, gradually add the whipping cream. Add the salt. Gradually add the cocoa powder, beating until the frosting is stiff enough to form peaks, 3 to 4 minutes longer, and until the chocolate is well blended.

Spread the frosting over the top and sides of the cake. Refrigerate for several hours before serving. Store any leftovers in the refrigerator.

Mexican Vanilla Ice Cream

For best results use a candy thermometer to measure the temperature of the milks and custard.

Makes 6 servings

Special Equipment

- Candy thermometer
- Ice cream freezer

1⅓ cups heavy cream

1⅓ cups whole milk

⅓ cup light corn syrup

½ cup plus 2 tablespoons sugar

¼ teaspoon salt

6 large egg yolks

6 teaspoons Mexican vanilla extract (see page 180)

2 teaspoons freshly ground cinnamon (optional)

Optional garnishes: chocolate syrup, fresh fruit, and chopped pecans or other nuts of your choice

In a medium saucepan over medium heat, combine the cream, milk, corn syrup, ¼ cup plus 2 tablespoons of the sugar, and the salt. Heat the mixture, stirring continuously, until the temperature reaches 170°F. Set aside off the heat.

In a medium bowl, use a whisk to blend the egg yolks and remaining ¼ cup sugar until the sugar dissolves and the yolks are light yellow in color.

Whisking constantly, add about 1 cup of the warm milk mixture slowly, pouring in a steady stream. If the hot milk is added too quickly, it may "scramble" the eggs and make the ice cream lumpy.

Stirring constantly, slowly add the blended egg yolk mixture to the hot milk in the saucepan. When well blended, return the saucepan to medium-low heat. Stirring constantly, heat to no more than 180°F. Stir in the vanilla and cinnamon, if using. Remove from the heat.

Into a small glass bowl, pour 1 cup of the custard mixture. Place this small bowl in the freezer for at least 4 hours.

Into a large glass bowl, pour the remaining custard. Cover with plastic wrap and refrigerate for at least 4 hours.

After at least 4 hours, add the small bowl of frozen custard to the large bowl of refrigerated custard. Use a large spoon or a rubber spatula to break up the frozen custard until it dissolves into the refrigerated portion. Stir gently.

Transfer all of the custard to a readied ice cream maker. Following the manufacturer's instructions, churn for 20 to 25 minutes, until the mixture thickens to the consistency of ice cream.

Into a medium baking pan, spoon the ice cream and place in the freezer for at least 1 hour before serving.

Garnish as desired and serve.

Tía Lupe's *Polvorones*

Small disc-shaped cookies known as *polvorones* are among my favorite Mexican sweets. These two-inch rounds are typically served on special occasions, especially birthdays, weddings, and major holidays.

This recipe is based on the cookies I remember my aunt, Tía Lupe, making. Well known for her *polvorones*, Tía Lupe sold her cinnamon sugar–sprinkled cookies all over the region for parties and big events. Although she did not share her prized recipe with me or anyone else, I experimented and experimented until I finally achieved the flavor and texture of her cookies.

This recipe calls for freshly ground Mexican cinnamon because it makes an appreciable difference in the flavor.

Makes 36 cookies

Vegetable oil or cooking spray
1 tablespoon (from 4 sticks) freshly ground Mexican cinnamon (see page 183), or regular ground cinnamon
3 cups all-purpose flour
1 cup sugar
2½ teaspoons baking powder
¼ teaspoon salt
2 cups vegetable shortening (Crisco preferred)
2 large eggs, lightly beaten
Mexican Cinnamon Sugar (see page 183)

Preheat oven to 350°F. Lightly coat a cookie sheet with oil or cooking spray.

In a large mixing bowl, combine the cinnamon, flour, sugar, baking powder, and salt. Using a large wooden spoon or your hands, blend the dry ingredients.

Using a pastry cutter, blend in the shortening until the mixture resembles coarsely ground cornmeal.

Add the eggs to the flour mixture. Using a spatula, blend well to make a smooth dough. Knead for about 1 minute.

Break off pieces of dough and roll to the size of a walnut. You should have about 36 pieces. Place the rounds of dough about 2 inches apart on the prepared cookie sheet. Press with your fingers and flatten to ½ inch thick. The cookies should be about 1 inch apart.

Bake for 15 to 20 minutes, until light golden on the bottom. Place the cookie sheet on a rack to cool for about 10 minutes.

Sprinkle the tops of the cookies with cinnamon sugar.

Store in an airtight container at room temperature for 1 week or freeze for up to 3 months.

Tía Lupe's *Polvorones* and Mexican Hot Chocolate (page 211).

Enchilada Queen *Sopapillas*

What's not to like about fried dough? *Sopapillas* are more New Mexico than Texas, like several other of my customers' favorite dishes, but I serve them by popular demand. Fresh out of the fryer, the fried pillows should be sprinkled with cinnamon sugar. I drizzle this very popular dessert with local honey or sauce it with Hershey's Chocolate Syrup to which I've added a touch of cinnamon.

Makes about 16 sopapillas

2¼ cups all-purpose flour

1 tablespoon baking powder

1 tablespoon sugar

¼ teaspoon salt

6 tablespoons unsalted butter, softened at room temperature

¾ cup very warm (110°F) water

1 quart vegetable oil or as needed

Cinnamon sugar (see page 183), as needed

1 cup local honey, or 1 cup Hershey's Chocolate Syrup mixed with 1 teaspoon ground cinnamon

In a large mixing bowl, combine the flour, baking powder, sugar, and salt. Blend well using your hands or a large spoon.

Using a pastry cutter or fork, combine the butter and flour mixture until well blended and crumbly.

Add the warm water and mix until the dough forms. Knead about 20 times, until smooth and elastic. Cover and set aside for at least 30 minutes to rest.

Pour oil into a deep-fryer or deep electric skillet, or a deep skillet or Dutch oven on the stovetop, to a depth of at least 2 inches. Heat the oil to 375°F.

Divide the dough into four portions.

On a floured board with a flour-dusted rolling pin, roll each portion of dough to about 8 inches square, about ⅛ inch thick. Sprinkle the surface lightly with flour to prevent sticking.

Using a knife, cut the dough square into four 4-inch squares or use a cookie cutter of about the same size.

Fry the *sopapillas* in batches in the hot oil for 15 to 20 seconds, until golden on one side. Using tongs or slotted spoon, turn and cook until golden on the other side, 15 to 20 seconds longer.

Using a slotted spoon, remove the *sopapilla*, allowing excess oil to drain back into the deep-fryer, to paper towels to absorb excess grease.

Sprinkle the tops of the warm sopapillas generously with cinnamon sugar.

Serve drizzled with honey or cinnamon chocolate syrup.

Frontera Capirotada
BREAD PUDDING

Tex-Mex *capirotada* (bread pudding) is an interesting combination of sweet and savory. This bread pudding has raisins, pecans, and coconut as well as two kinds of cheese. During my childhood, the only time my mother and grandmother would make *capirotada* was during Lent. I love it any time of year.

Many Mexican cooks just south of the border use peanuts instead of pecans, and others prefer *queso fresco* instead of Chihuahua or Monterey Jack cheese. Just north of the border, yellow cheese is the traditional choice.

For my recipe, I use both white and yellow cheeses to capture the flavors of *capirotada*s from both sides of the Rio Grande. I also use *piloncillo*, a form of minimally processed sugar sold in cone shapes, typically found in Hispanic markets. You may substitute dark brown sugar but you will miss out on the hint of rum flavor and smoky, earthy accents.

Traditionally, *capirotada* is served hot or warm. But I'm just as happy to eat it at room temperature or chilled. Refrigerate any leftovers and reheat gently in a microwave oven.

Makes 12 servings

1 (24-ounce) loaf split-top, thick-sliced supermarket white bread
1 cup grated *piloncillo* (brown sugar cone available in Hispanic markets, see page 194), or 1 cup dark brown sugar
1 teaspoon anise seeds
1 (4-inch) cinnamon stick
1 cup raisins
1 cup pecan pieces
½ cup sweetened flaked coconut
1½ cups shredded cheddar cheese
1½ cups shredded Chihuahua or Monterey Jack cheese
Ground cinnamon (optional)

Preheat the oven to 350°F. Butter the bottom and sides of a 9 × 13-inch glass baking dish or metal baking pan.

Cut the bread into 1-inch squares.

On a large baking sheet, spread the bread squares in a single layer. Bake for about 10 minutes to toast the bread to a golden brown. Halfway through the baking time, turn the bread to toast the other side. Set aside off the heat.

In a large saucepan or stockpot over high heat, combine the *piloncillo*, anise, cinnamon stick, and 6½ cups water. Bring to a boil, then reduce the heat and simmer for about 10 minutes. Set aside off the heat for about 5 minutes.

Pour the *piloncillo* liquid through a fine strainer to remove the solids, reserving the liquid. Add the raisins to the liquid, cover, and set aside for 5 to 10 minutes to plump raisins.

Place half the toasted bread in the bottom of the prepared baking dish. Again pour the *piloncillo* liquid through a fine strainer, reserving the liquid and raisins separately.

Pour about half of the liquid over the bread, making certain the bread is completely soaked. Sprinkle half the soaked raisins and half of the pecans over the bread. Evenly distribute all the coconut over the raisins and pecans. Layer ¾ cup each of the cheeses over the coconut. Spread the remaining bread pieces over all.

Pour the remaining liquid over the bread, making certain the bread is completely soaked. Sprinkle the remaining raisins and pecans over the bread. Top all with the remaining cheeses.

Cover with foil and bake for about 25 minutes, until the mixture has puffed.

Remove the foil and set aside to cool for about 15 minutes before serving.

Sprinkle with cinnamon before serving, if desired.

How to work with piloncillo cones

Use a box grater or microplane to grate *piloncillo*. This form of sugar is very hard. Cutting the cone into pieces requires a heavy cleaver or strong serrated knife and some strength. Sometimes I put it in a bag and hit it with a hammer to break it into smaller pieces for grating.

South Texas *Buñuelos*

Buñuelos are the Rio Grande preference for edible good luck insurance on New Year's Day. I'd much rather rely on these fried treats than black-eyed peas, eaten around the rest of the state and the South, for luck to start the New Year. My mom and grandmother always fried *buñuelos* on New Year's Eve. I made sure to eat one for dessert, snack, and breakfast the next day, if they lasted that long. I wanted to be sure I had plenty of good luck coming my way.

Though the dough is similar to that of *sopapillas*, *buñuelos* are thinner and crispier. They have cinnamon in the dough and get a sprinkling of cinnamon sugar on top. Make sure *buñuelos* are rolled very thin so they fry up crispy.

Makes 18 bunelos

2 cups all-purpose flour
2 teaspoons baking powder
2 teaspoons sugar
½ teaspoon ground cinnamon
¼ teaspoon salt
¼ cup vegetable shortening
¾ cup very warm (110°F) water
3 cups vegetable oil
Cinnamon sugar (see page 183)

In a medium bowl, combine the flour, baking powder, sugar, cinnamon, and salt. Using your hands or a large wooden spoon, blend well.

Using a pastry cutter or fork, blend in the shortening until it is well mixed.

Add the warm water; gently blend all the ingredients until they all come together. Knead no more than 20 times to form a smooth dough.

Cover with plastic wrap and a clean towel and set aside for 30 minutes to 1 hour.

Knead once or twice, then break off pieces of dough and shape slightly smaller than a golf ball. You should have 18 balls of dough.

On a floured board with a flour-dusted rolling pin, roll each ball into a very thin circle, about ⅛ inch. *Buñuelos* should be about 6 inches in diameter when rolled thin enough.

In a large saucepan or deep-fryer, heat the oil to 365°F. Carefully slip the *buñuelos* one at a time into the hot oil. Fry each until golden brown and crisp, 2 to 3 minutes, turning once or basting with hot oil to fry the top. Remove to paper towels to drain. Keep warm.

Sprinkle cinnamon sugar on the *buñuelos*. Serve warm or at room temperature.

Pumpkin *Empanadas*

This is another recipe for homemade nostalgia. These sweet baked turnovers recall fabulous memories of my mother's and grandmother's baking. Like many of their special treats, these treasures were more often prepared during the cooler months, especially in November, around Thanksgiving. As a young mother and homemaker, I created a recipe to prepare in my home for my children. I have even made them with apples and cinnamon. No matter the filling, they're delicious, inside and out.

Makes 18 empanadas

Dough

2¼ cups all-purpose flour, or more if needed

¼ cup sugar

1 tablespoon baking powder

2 teaspoons ground cinnamon

¼ teaspoon salt

½ cup vegetable shortening

1 cup very warm (110°F) milk, or more if needed

Pumpkin Filling

2 (15-ounce) cans solid pack pumpkin (not pumpkin pie filling)

¼ cup brown sugar

2 teaspoons ground cinnamon

Preheat the oven to 375°F. Spray a baking sheet with cooking spray.

Make the dough: In a large mixing bowl, combine the flour, sugar, baking powder, cinnamon, and salt, blending well with a whisk.

Using a pastry blender, mix in the shortening and evenly blend all the ingredients. Add the warm milk and knead for about 1 minute. Do not overwork the dough. If the dough is stiff, add 1 tablespoon more milk. If the dough is sticky, add 1 tablespoon flour or until the dough is smooth and does not stick.

Break off pieces of dough and shape slightly smaller than a golf ball. You should have 18 balls of dough. Cover the dough balls with plastic wrap and allow to rest for about 1 hour.

Make the pumpkin filling: In a medium bowl using an electric mixer, blend the pumpkin, brown sugar, and cinnamon until the brown sugar dissolves and the ingredients are well blended. Set aside.

Lightly sprinkle flour on a pastry or cutting board. Using a rolling pin, roll each ball to about 3 inches in diameter.

Place 2 scant tablespoons of the filling in the center of each circle.

Fold over, making sure the edges are even all the way around. Pinch together the edges to seal the empanada. An alternative method is to press the edges with a fork.

Place the empanadas on the prepared baking sheet and bake for about 15 minutes, until the dough is golden in color. Serve warm or at room temperature.

CHAPTER 11

SIPPING WITH THE ENCHILADA QUEEN

No doubt the margarita is the ultimate Tex-Mex cocktail. In recent years, however, fresh fruit juices, known as *aguas*—traditionally sold from street carts in Mexico and snow cone stands in many Texas border towns—have become wildly popular as well. In the past ten years, little snow cone stands have cropped up all over the border area. The growing popularity of *aguas* once again proves the adage: "Mexican Food only travels north." Sweet and refreshing, these drinks are consumed daily to quench thirsts on hot, often dusty, streets.

Just as traditional, Mexican Hot Chocolate (page 211) is a winter comfort. Although snow is a rarity, border towns do get cold in the winter, and a cup of steaming chocolate is a fine tribute to the Maya and Aztecs who brought us chocolate in the first place.

The beverages in this chapter are not a compendium of Tex-Mex sipping. Rather they are my favorites and the drinks that I feel reflect the tastes of *la frontera*.

The Perfect Margarita

Made to order with fresh lime juice, the Enchilada Queen's margarita recipe is a huge favorite in our bar and in my home. Of course, the higher quality the tequila, the smoother the flavor! When making margaritas with premium aged tequila known as *añejo*, we use top-quality Grand Marnier, orange brandy. With *reposado* tequila, we use high-quality but slightly less expensive triple sec, orange-flavored liqueur. Our house margarita is made with good-quality silver tequila and agave nectar.

To salt the rim of a margarita glass

Moisten the rim with a wedge of lime, then press
the rim into a thin layer of kosher salt.

Bar (Simple) Syrup

It's not called simple for nothing. It could also be called Handy Syrup. Indispensable for making cocktails, this mixture of water and sugar also works well in iced tea. No more undissolved sugar at the bottom of the glass. Use the same ratio as teaspoons of sugar.

Makes 1 cup

1 cup granulated sugar
1 cup cold water

In a medium saucepan over medium-high heat, combine the sugar and water, stirring to dissolve the sugar. Bring to a boil, then reduce the heat to low, stirring constantly until the sugar dissolves completely and the mixture is clear, 3 to 5 minutes.

Let cool completely before using.

Store at room temperature in container with tight-fitting lid.

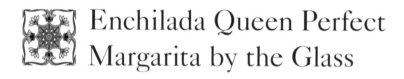

Enchilada Queen Perfect Margarita by the Glass

When making a Perfect Margarita, shake well with ice in a cocktail shaker, then strain into a chilled glass. Or serve with ice "on the rocks."

Makes 1 cocktail

Kosher salt or granulated sugar
  (optional)
1½ ounces tequila (*añejo,
  reposado,* or silver)
1 ounce orange brandy (Grand
  Marnier) or liqueur (triple sec)
1 ounce fresh lime juice
1 ounce agave nectar or Bar
  (Simple) Syrup (see opposite)
Lime wedge

If desired, rim 6 chilled margarita or cocktail glasses with kosher salt or sugar (see opposite). Set aside.

In a cocktail shaker with ice, combine the tequila, orange brandy, lime juice, and agave nectar.

Shake the container well, 6 or 7 times, and pour through the shaker strainer into the chilled glass. Garnish with a wedge of lime.

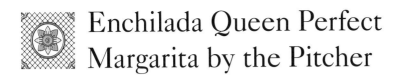

Enchilada Queen Perfect Margarita by the Pitcher

For parties, making margaritas by the pitcher makes good sense. Here's the formula.

Makes 6 cocktails

Kosher salt or granulated sugar
   (optional)
12 ounces (1½ cups) tequila
   (*añejo*, *reposado*, or silver)
8 ounces (1 cup) orange brandy
   (Grand Marnier) or liqueur
   (triple sec)
8 ounces (1 cup) fresh lime juice
8 ounces (1 cup) agave nectar or
   Bar (Simple) Syrup (page 200)
6 lime wedges

If desired, rim six chilled margarita or cocktail glasses with kosher salt or sugar (see page 200). Set aside.

In a pitcher, combine the tequila, orange brandy, lime juice, and agave nectar, stirring to blend.

Refrigerate for about 2 hours before serving.

Serve the margaritas in the chilled glasses. Garnish with wedges of lime.

Ruby Red Margaritas by the Pitcher

Makes 6 cocktails

Kosher salt or granulated sugar
  (optional)
12 ounces (1½ cups) silver
  tequila, chilled
12 ounces (1½ cups) fresh ruby
  red grapefruit juice, chilled
6 ounces (¾ cup) fresh lime
  juice, chilled
3 ounces triple sec
3 ounces agave nectar
Lime slice(s) (optional)

In a 1-gallon container or pitcher with a a lid, combine the tequila, grapefruit and lime juices, triple sec, and agave nectar. Stir (or shake) well and serve up (without ice) or on the rocks (over fresh ice) in the chilled glasses.

Garnish with lime slices, if desired.

If desired, rim six chilled margarita or cocktail glasses with kosher salt or sugar (see page 200). Set aside.

Ruby Red Margarita by the Glass

My dad looked after a big ruby red grapefruit tree in the back of our house. He also had an orange tree, but it was the grapefruit that flourished. Our backyard grapefruit tree produced so much fruit that we had plenty to give away to neighbors. For me, grapefruit means bounty and sharing.

Like all varieties of grapefruit, the ruby red, a Texas-bred hybrid that thrives in the Lower Rio Grande Valley, delivers plenty of vitamins C and A. Combining good nutrition with a fun cocktail equals a win-win. The ruby red also delivers a bonus in that it is a good source of the nutrient lycopene, the substance that gives the ruby red its distinctive color. Lycopene does more than make ruby red grapefruit beautiful, however. It is a robust antioxidant, making ruby red grapefruit juice healthful as well as lovely.

Makes 1 cocktail

Kosher salt or granulated sugar (optional)
2 ounces silver tequila
2 ounces fresh ruby red grapefruit juice
1 ounce fresh lime juice
½ ounce triple sec
½ ounce agave nectar
Lime slice(s) (optional)

If desired, rim a chilled margarita or cocktail glass with kosher salt or sugar (see page 200). Set aside.

Fill a cocktail shaker with ice cubes. Pour the tequila, grapefruit and lime juices, triple sec, and agave nectar over ice. Cover and shake to blend well.

Strain and serve up (without ice) or on the rocks (over fresh ice) in the chilled glass.

Garnish with lime slices, if desired.

Mango Margarita

In the bar at my restaurants, we offer fine boutique tequilas, new on the market, as well as classic brands. My favorite way to drink tequila is straight up on the rocks. I generally prefer *añejo* or *reposado*, sipped very slowly. But when it is margarita time, this is my favorite frozen margarita, made with fresh fruit and juice.

Makes 1 cocktail

1½ ounces tequila

1½ ounces orange liqueur such as triple sec or Cointreau

¼ cup chopped fresh mango

½ cup fresh orange juice

Juice of ½ lime

1 cup crushed ice

1 or more lime wedges

In a blender jar, combine the tequila, orange liqueur, mango, orange and lime juices, and ice. Process until slushy, about 1 minute.

Serve in a chilled glass rimmed with kosher salt (see page 200), if desired. Garnish with a lime wedge or two.

Abundio's Prized Sangria

One of my general managers, Abundio Reyes, created this sangria, first for his family's special events. We started serving it, and customers love it. So do I. The flavors are very refreshing and balanced. Since the recipe begins with a prepared sangria (we use Yago brand), it is very simple to put together, chill, and serve. We also use an economical brandy, Presidente brand. This travels well for tailgating and picnicking.

Makes about 20 (6-ounce) servings

3 quarts Yago Sangria Wine

½ cup sugar

12 ounces (1½ cups) brandy

12 ounces (1½ cups) fresh
   orange juice

6 ounces (¾ cup) fresh lime
   juice

1 orange, unpeeled and cut into
   ⅛-inch-thick slices

1 lime, unpeeled and cut into
   ⅛-inch-thick slices

In a large (1-gallon) container or pitcher, combine 2 cups of the sangria wine with the sugar, stirring well to dissolve the sugar.

Add the remaining sangria, the brandy, and orange and lime juices. Stir or shake well with the lid tightly closed to combine the ingredients.

Chill for several hours in refrigerator.

Serve in wineglasses, tumblers, or plastic cups over ice, garnished with slices of orange and lime.

Aguas Frescas (Mexican Fruit Juice Drinks)

Aguas have become very popular in recent years. We serve a variety of *aguas* at the restaurants for brunch. As a kid, I drank them when we went across the border to Matamoros and bought them at the *mercado*.

Agua de Sandía
WATERMELON JUICE DRINK

I love watermelon, and this is one of my very favorite *agua* recipes. When we serve *Agua de Sandía* for Sylvia's Enchilada Kitchen brunch, we have to make extra since our customers go back for seconds and thirds.

Makes 1½ gallons

4 quarts cubed seedless
    watermelon
3½ cups cold water
Up to 1½ cups sugar
12 cups ice cubes

Place batches of watermelon in a blender, add cold water to the top of the fruit, and puree until smooth, about 1 minute. Continue to process until all the fruit is blended with 3½ cups cold water.

Pour the blended watermelon into a 2-gallon pitcher. Add ½ to ¾ cup sugar. Taste and add more sugar, if desired. Refrigerate until very cold before serving.

To serve, half fill a clean 2-gallon pitcher with ice. Pour the watermelon juice drink over the ice. Serve immediately.

Enchilada Queen Refreshing
Agua de Límon

LIMEADE

You may think *Agua de Límon* is lemonade, but you'd be wrong. Remember, *límon* means lime, and Mexicans think of lemons as yellow limes. Limeade is one of the favorite *aguas* served in Mexico and one I keep on hand at home and at the restaurant as a refresher.

When ordering this drink in many *frontera* restaurants, you get a choice between still water and *agua mineral*. I like the fizz of club soda or sparkling water and the flavor boost of lime zest. The oils in the outer peel of limes—the zest—really adds flavor zing, whether you use sparkling or uncarbonated water.

Makes ½ gallon

6 large limes
1 liter club soda, chilled
1½ cups sugar, or more to taste
4 cups ice

Using a zester or microplane, grate the green outer zest of the limes. Set aside.

Cut the limes and squeeze all the juice from each lime. Pour the lime juice into a 1-gallon container.

Add the chilled club soda, lime zest, and sugar. Stir well to dissolve the sugar.

Add the ice and more sugar, if desired.

Mexican Hot Chocolate

The two favorite brands of Mexican hot chocolate, Ibarra and Abuelita, are sold as chocolate "tablets." Both, flavored with cinnamon, are so very homey on a cold day. Traditionally, Mexican hot chocolate drinks were aerated with a *molinero*, which is wooden tool, sort of like a whisk, placed in the chocolate and twirled between the palms of your hands to blend and aerate the hot chocolate. Today, I use an electric mixer.

Mexican Hot Chocolate

My mom and grandmother prepared this warm and cozy drink for breakfast.

Makes 4 servings

1 tablet Mexican hot chocolate
   (Abuelita or Ibarra)
2 (4-inch) cinnamon sticks
4 cups whole milk

In a medium saucepan over low heat, melt the chocolate tablet in ¼ cup water, stirring constantly.

Add the milk and cinnamon sticks. Raise the heat to medium-high, stirring frequently until the milk foams. Remove from the heat as soon as the milk begins to foam. Do not boil.

Using a handheld electric mixer, beat on high speed for 15 to 30 seconds, until the milk froths. Serve immediately.

Sylvia Casares standing on a sand dune at Boca Chica Beach, where the Rio Grande empties into the Gulf of Mexico. The sand bar behind Sylvia is in Mexico! This stretch of federal land is protected from development. Its raw beauty is the same as when Sylvia visited this spot as a child.

RESOURCE LIST

There are some ingredients called for in border cooking that you may not be familiar with or may not be available if you don't live in the Southwest or in a place with a large Latin community. If Mexican spices and dried chiles aren't readily available, the Internet is a good source.

- Abuelita chocolate (see page 211) is a tradition in many Hispanic homes and widely available in supermarkets. It is also available on the Nestlé website: www.nestleusa.com/brands/drinks/abuelita.

- Beef base adds body and flavor to *Caldo de Res* (page 123). Better than Bouillon beef base is recommended: www.betterthanbouillon.com/products.

- Blue Cattle Truck Mexican Vanilla (page 180) is the Cadillac of Mexican vanillas and a reliable source: www.mexicanvanilla.com.

- Bolner's Fiesta Brand Spices in San Antonio sells a wide variety of Mexican herbs and spices, also corn husks: www.fiestaspices.com.

- *Cabrito* (baby goat) (page 115) is much more widely available today than it used to be, in part because of its popularity in communities with Hispanic and halal (Muslim) markets. Elkusa.com is a good Internet source as well: www.elkusa.com/Goat_meat.

- Chicken base made by Knorr (see page 121) is a favorite flavor enhancer for Hispanic cooks: www.knorr.com/product/category/949134/latin-flavors. If Knorr brand is unavailable, any quality brand of chicken base will do the job; try Better than Bouillon: www.betterthanbouillon.com/products.

- *María galletas* tea biscuits or cookies are available in the Hispanic foods section of many supermarkets, and online: mexgrocer.com.

- Melissa's Produce offers an excellent selection of Hispanic produce and ingredients, especially dried chiles: http://www.melissas.com.

- Mexican herbs and spices, along with many other products, can be purchased at Mexgrocer: http://www.mexgrocer.com/catagories-spices---herbs.

- Texas ruby red grapefruit can be ordered from Texas Sweet: www.texasweet.com/texas-grapefruits-and-oranges.

- White Wings flour and mixes for tortillas (page 15) are the Rio Grande brand of choice, especially in South Texas: http://whitewingsbrand.com.

ACKNOWLEDGMENTS

To Elizabeth Beier, my editor at St. Martin's Press, who honored me and my cooking by giving me the chance to share my recipes with all lovers of this cuisine. Elizabeth's expert palate and publishing wisdom have been a gift to me.

To my *Camotes* (Sweet Potatoes, which is a South Texas term for very near and dear trusted friends) Dedie Leahy, my literary agent, and Dotty Griffith, my writer—the priceless wisdom, loyalty, skills, and experience of you both have been a treasure to this project.

To my children, Jason, Celeste, and, especially, Nick, who dropped everything he was doing and managed my restaurants at a time when I needed that help so much.

To Oscar, my brother, who came to my rescue with marketing and advertising direction during the early years of Sylvia's and continues to do so—and who wrote the beautiful foreword to this book. To my brothers, Noel and Idoluis, and all my family who did so much to help me.

To Don Guggenheim, who has helped me with the management of my restaurants so I could focus on my book.

To my loyal customers, who have supported me and advocated for my restaurants and whose prayers and support made all the difference.

To my loyal employees who have stayed with me through great times and challenging times.

To my dearest friends, who have supported me through thick and thin: you are too many to name and too important to leave out. I thank you all from the bottom of my heart.

My family at the wedding of my daughter, Celeste, in Houston, on March 26, 2013.
To my right is my oldest son, Jason, and his wife, Mary Beth. To my left are Celeste, Mark,
and Nick. In front of me are my grandchildren, David and Beth.

INDEX